D0823420

Sri Swami Sivananda
(1887-1963)

Autobiography

of

SWAMI SIVANANDA

Published By

THE DIVINE LIFE SOCIETY
P.O. SHIVANANDANAGAR—249 192
Distt. Tehri-Garhwal, U.P., Himalayas, India

Price]   1995   [Rs. 45/-

Sixth Edition: 1995
(4,000 Copies)

ISBN 81-7052-029-0

Published by Swami Krishnananda for The Divine Life Society,
Shivanandanagar, and printed by him at the Yoga-Vedanta Forest
Academy Press, P.O. Shivanandanagar, Distt. Tehri-Garhwal, U.P.,
Himalayas, India

PUBLISHERS' NOTE

A saint's life is the ideal for all to emulate, a pattern for everyone who would make his own life sublime. It is an open book from which to learn the lessons of divine life. However much one tries to gain knowledge of spiritual truths from scriptures and texts, it is not until one actually sees someone in whom those truths shine exemplified that one is ready, willing and eager to realise those truths in actual daily life.

That is the purpose that this inspiring book serves.

THE DIVINE LIFE SOCIETY

शिवानन्दस्तुतिः

(Sri Swami Jnanananda)

(१) मायाकूपारमग्नानवशजनगणान् त्रातुकामं प्रकामं
कायायासावसादं सकलमपि तृणीकृत्य कृत्यप्रसक्तम्
छायानाथोपमामं सुचिरमतिमुदाऽभ्यस्तयोगासनादि-
व्यायामावाप्तसत्त्वं शिवमनवरतं भावये योगिवर्यम्

(२) नानालोकाय नित्यं प्रतिपदमधुरं शान्तिसन्देशपत्रं
पीनामोदप्रवाहप्रगुणितकरुणं प्रेषयन्तं महान्तम्
मानातीतप्रभावं मनसि मनसिजारातिमालोक्य गाढं
ध्यानाविष्टं प्रकृष्टप्रकृतिगुणयुतं श्री शिवानन्दमीडे

(३) विश्वाराध्यं विशिष्टप्रतिभमभयदं प्राणिनामाश्रितानां
विश्वासामत्रमार्तिप्रशमननिरतं साधुलोकावलम्बम्
विश्वाधीशप्रभावं भृशमखिलजनान् बोधयित्वाऽऽर्षधम
शश्वत् संस्थापयन्तं शिवमुनिमनिशं भावये दिव्यरूपम्

(४) वेदान्तांभोधिगर्मादिविरलविलसत्तत्त्वरत्नान्यजस्रं
मोदादुद्धृत्य नानामनुजगुणगणायान्वहं दातुकामम्
खेदावेशावशानाममितसुखकरं नित्यकल्याणरंगं
श्रीदानोत्कं मुनीन्द्रं शिवमखिलजगदेशिकं भावयेऽहम्

SIVA'S EXPERIENCE

1. I have seen God in my own Self.

2. I have negated name and form, and what remains is Existence-Knowledge-Bliss Absolute and nothing else.

3. I behold God everywhere. There is no veil.

4. I am One. There is no duality.

5. I rest in my own Self. My bliss is beyond description.

6. The world of dreams has gone. I alone exist.

Swami Sivananda

SIVA'S MESSAGE

Delight in good.

Make up your mind to tread the spiritual path.

Be patient.

Go slowly. Go ahead.

Be deliberate.

Assert.

Recognize.

Realise: *I am the immortal Soul.*

This is the discipline.

This is Siva's message.

Swami Sivananda

HOW GOD CAME INTO MY LIFE

(Swami Sivananda)

It would be easy to dismiss the question by saying: "Yes, after a prolonged period of intense austerities and meditation, while I was living at Swaragashram and when I had the Darshan and blessings of a number of Maharishis, the Lord appeared before me in the form of Sri Krishna.

But that would not be the whole truth, nor a sufficient answer to a question relating to God, who is infinite, unlimited and beyond the reach of speech and mind.

Cosmic Consciousness is not an accident or chance. It is the summit, accessible by a thorny path that has steps—slippery steps. I ascended them step by step the hard way; but at every stage I experienced God coming into my life and lifting me easily to the next stage.

My father was fond of ceremonial worship in which he was very regular. To my child-mind the image he worshipped was God, and I delighted in helping father in the worship by bringing him flowers and other articles of worship. The deep inner satisfaction that he and I derived from such worship implanted in my heart a strong conviction that God was in such images devoutly worshipped by His devotees. Thus did God first come into my life and place my foot on the first rung of the spiritual ladder.

As an adult I was fond of gymnastics and vigorous

exercises. I learnt fencing from a teacher who belonged to a low caste. He was a Harijan. I could go to him only for a few days before I was made to understand that it was unbecoming of a caste-Brahmin to play the student to an untouchable. I thought deeply over the matter. One moment I felt that the God whom we worshipped in the image in my father's worship room had jumped over to the heart of this untouchable. He was my Guru all right. So I immediately went to him with flowers, sweets and clothes and garlanded him, placed flowers at his feet and prostrated myself before him. Thus did God come into my life to remove the veil of caste distinctions.

How very valuable this step was I could realise soon after this, for i was to enter the medical profession and serve all, and the persistence of caste distinctions would have made that service a mockery. With this mist cleared by the light of God, it was easy and natural for me to serve everyone. I took keen delight in every kind of service connected with the healing and alleviation of human misery. If there was a good prescription for malaria, I felt that the whole world should know it the next moment. Any knowledge about the prevention of diseases, promotion of health and healing of diseases I was eager to acquire and share with all.

Then in Malaya, God came to me in the form of the sick. It is difficult for me now to single out any instance, and perhaps it is unnecessary. Time and space are concepts of the mind and have no meaning in God. I can look back now upon the whole period of my stay in Malaya as a single event in which God came to me in the form of the sick and suffering. People are sick physically and mentally. To some, life is lingering death; and to

X

others, death is more welcome than life; some invite death and commit suicide, unable to face life.

The aspiration grew within me that if God had not made this world merely as a hell where wicked people would be thrown to suffer, and if there is (as I intuitively felt there should be) something other than this misery and this helpless existence, it should be known well and experienced.

It was at this crucial point in my life that God came to me as a religious mendicant who gave me the first lesson in Vedanta. The positive aspects of life here and the real end and aim of human life were made apparent. This drew me from Malaya to the Himalaya. God now came to me in the form of an all-consuming aspiration to realise Him as the Self of all.

Meditation and service went apace; and then came various spiritual experiences. The body, mind and intellect as the limiting adjuncts, vanished, and the whole universe shone as His Light. God then came in the form of this Light in which everything assumed a divine shape and the pain and suffering that seem to haunt everybody appeared to be a mirage, the illusion that ignorance creates on account of low sensual appetites that lurk in man.

One more milestone had to be passed in order to know that "everything is Brahman." Early in 1950 — on the 8th of January — the Lord came to me in the form of a half-demented assailant, who disturbed the night Satsang at the Ashram. His attempt failed. I bowed to him, worshipped him and sent him home. Evil exists in order to glorify the good. Evil is a superficial appearance. Beneath its veil the one Self shines in all.

A noteworthy fact ought to be mentioned here. In this evolution nothing gained previously was entirely discarded at any later stage. One coalesced into the next, and the Yoga of Synthesis was the fruit. Idol-worship, service of the sick, practice of meditation, the cultivation of cosmic love that transcended the barriers of caste, creed and religion, with the ultimate aim of attaining the state of Cosmic Consciousness, was revealed. This knowledge had to be shared immediately. All this had to become an integral part of my being.

The mission had been gathering strength and spreading. It was in 1951 that I undertook the All-India Tour. Then God came to me in His Virat-Swarupa—as multitudes of devotees—eager to listen to the tenets of divine life. At every centre I felt that God spoke through me, and He Himself in His cosmic form spread out before me as the multitude, listened to me. He sang with me, He prayed with me; He spoke and He also listened. "Sarvam Khalvidam Brahma—all indeed is Brahman."

WHAT LIFE HAS TAUGHT ME

(Swami Sivananda)

it was, i should say, by a flash that i came to the conclusion early in my life that human life is not complete with its observable activities and that there is something above human perception controlling and directing all that is visible. I may boldly say that I began to perceive the realities behind what we call life on earth. The unrest and feverish anxiety that characterise man's ordinary existence here bespeak a higher goal that he has to reach one day or the other.

When man gets entangled in selfishness, greed, hatred and lust, he naturally forgets what is beneath his own skin. Materialism and scepticism reign supreme. He gets irritated over little things and begins to fight and quarrel; in short, man becomes miserable.

The doctor's profession gave me ample evidence of the great sufferings of this world. I was blessed with a new vision and perspective. I was deeply convinced that there must be a place—a sweet home of pristine glory, purity and divine splendour—where absolute security, perfect peace and happiness can be enjoyed eternally. Therefore, in conformity with the dictum of the *Sruti*, I renounced the world—and felt that I now belonged to the whole world.

A course of severe self-discipline and penance endowed me with enough strength to move unscathed amidst the vicissitudes of the world-phenomena. And I began to feel the great good it would do to humanity if I could share this new vision with one and all. I called my instrument of work "The Divine Life Society."

Side by side, the stirring events since the advent of the twentieth century, had their effects upon all keen-minded people. The horrors of the past and possible wars, and the consequent suffering, touched the minds of people. It was not difficult to see that the pains of mankind were mostly brought on by its own deeds. To awaken man to his errors and follies, and to make him mend his ways so that he may utilise his life for attaining worthier ends, was felt to be the urgent need of the time. As if in answer to this need, I saw the birth of the Divine Life Mission, with its task of rescuing man from the forces of the lower nature and raising him to the consciousness of his true relationship with the Cosmos. This is the work of rousing the religious consciousness, of bringing man to an awareness of his essential divinity.

Not by mere argument or discussion can religion be taught or understood. Not by precepts or canons of teaching alone can you make one religious. It requires a peculiar atonement with one's vast enviromnent, an ability to feel the deepest as well as the vastest. It requires a genuine sympathy with creation. Religion is living, not speaking or showing. I hold that whatever be one's religion, whoever be the prophet one adores, whatever be one's language or country, age or sex, one can be religious provided the true implication of that hallowed term "Tapas," which essentially means any form of self-control, is made capable of being practised in daily

xiv

life to the extent possible for one, in the environment and under the circumstances in which one is placed.

I hold that real religion is the religion of the heart. The heart must be purified first. Truth, love and purity are the basis of real religion. Control over the baser nature, conquest of the mind, cultivation of virtues, service of humanity, goodwill, fellowship and amity, constitute the fundamentals of true religion. These ideals are included in the principles of the Divine Life Society. And I try to teach them mostly by example, which I consider to be weightier than all precepts.

The modern thinker has neither the requisite time nor the patience to perform rigorous Tapas and austere religious practices; and many of these are even being relegated to the level of superstition. In order to give the present generation the benefit of real Tapas in the true religious sense, to reveal to them its real significance, and to convince them of its meaning and efficacy, I hold up my torch of divine life, which is a system of religious life suited to one and all, which can be practised by the recluse and the office-goer alike, which is intelligible to the scholar and the rustic, in its different stages and phases. This is a religion which is not other than what is essential to give true meaning to the daily duties of the human being.

The beauty of divine life is its simplicity and applicability to the everyday affairs of the ordinary man. It is immaterial whether one goes to the church or the mosque or the temple for offering one's prayers, for all sincere prayers are heard by the Divine.

The average seeker after Truth is very often deceived

by the caprices of his mind. A person who takes to the spiritual path is bewildered before he reaches the end of his journey. He is naturally tempted to relax his efforts half-way. Many are the pitfalls, but those who plod on steadily are sure to reach the goal of life, which is universality of being, knowledge and joy. I have laid great emphasis in all my writings upon the discipline of the turbulent senses, conquest of the mind, purification of the heart, and attainment of inner peace and strength, suited to the different stages in evolution.

I have understood that it is the foremost duty of man to learn to give, to give in charity, to give in plenty, to give with love and without expectation of any reward, because one does not lose anything by giving, — on the other hand the giver is given back a thousandfold. Charity is not merely an act of offering certain material goods, for charity is incomplete without charity of disposition, of feeling, and of understanding and knowledge. Charity is self-sacrifice in the different levels of one's being. Charity in the highest sense I understand to be equivalent to Jnana Yajna, the sacrifice of wisdom.

Similarly, I consider that goodness of being and doing constitute the rock-bottom of one's life. By goodness I mean the capacity to feel with others and to live and feel as others do, and be in a position to act so that no one is hurt by the act. Goodness is the face of Godliness. I think that to be good in reality, in the innermost recesses of one's heart, is not easy, though it may appear to be simple as a teaching. It is one of the hardest things on earth, if only one would be honest with oneself.

There is no physical world for me. What I see I see

xvi

as the glorious manifestation of the Almighty. I rejoice when I behold the Purusha with thousands of heads and thousands of eyes and feet, that Sahasrarasirsha Purusha. When I serve persons, I see not the persons, but Him of whom they are the limbs. I learn to be humble before the mighty Being whose breath we breathe and whose joy we enjoy. I do not think there is anything more to teach or to learn. Here is the cream of religion, the quintessence of philosophy that anyone really needs.

The philosophy I hold is neither a dreamy, subjective, world-negating doctrine of illusion, nor a crude world-affirming theory of sense-ridden humanism. It is the fact of the divinity of the universe, the immortality of the soul of man, the unity of creation with the Absolute, that I feel is the only doctrine worth considering. As the one all-pervading Brahman appears as the diverse universe in all the planes of its manifestation, the aspirant has to pay his homage to the lower manifestations before he steps into the higher.

Sound health, clear understanding, deep knowledge, a pure, powerful will and moral integrity, are all necessary parts of the process of the realisation of the ideal of humanity as a whole.

To adjust, adapt and accommodate, to see good in everything, to bring to effective use all the principles of nature in the process of evolution towards Self-realisation along the path of an integrated adjustment of the human powers and faculties, are some of the main factors that go to build up a philosophy of life. To me, philosophy is not merely a love of wisdom, but actual possession of it. In all my writings I have prescribed methods for overcoming and mastering the physical, intellectual, mental and vital layers of consciousness, in order to be able to proceed with the Sadhana for self-perfection.

To behold the Lord in every being or form, to feel Him everywhere, at all times and in all conditions of life, to see, hear, taste and feel everything as God, is my creed.

To live in God, to melt in God, and to dissolve in God, is my creed.

By dwelling in such union, to utilise the hands, mind, senses and the body in the service of humanity, to sing the Names of the Lord, to elevate devotees, to give instructions to sincere aspirants, and disseminate knowledge throughout the world, is my creed, if you can call it one.

To be a cosmic friend and cosmic benefactor, a friend of the poor, the forlorn, the helpless and the fallen, is my creed.

It is my sacred creed to serve the sick, to nurse them with care, sympathy and love, to cheer up the depressed, to infuse power and joy in all, to feel oneness with each and everyone, and to treat all with equal vision.

In my highest creed there are neither peasants nor kings, neither beggars nor emperors, neither males nor females, neither teachers nor students. I love to live, move and have my being in this realm indescribable.

The first step is often the most difficult one. But once it is taken the rest becomes easy. There is a need for more courage and patience on the part of people. They usually shirk, hesitate and are frightened. All this is due to ignorance of one's true duty. A certain amount of education and culture is necessary to have a sufficiently clear grasp of one's position in this world. Our educational system needs an overhaul, for it is now floating on the surface without touching the depths of man. To achieve this, cooperation should come not only from society but also from the government.

Success is difficult without mutual help. The head and heart should go hand in hand, and the ideal and the reality should have a close relation. To work with this knowledge is Karma Yoga. The Lord has declared this truth in the *Bhagavad Gita*.

I pray that this supreme ideal be actualised in the daily life of every individual. I pray that there be heaven on earth. This is not merely a wish, – this is a possibility and a fact that cannot be gainsaid. It is to be realised if life is to mean what it ought to mean.

INTRODUCTION

(Swami Sadananda Saraswati)

When I received the set of manuscripts bearing the title *Autobiography of Swami Sivananda*, I jumped with joy because I expected, as I believe many would expect, that there was a chance to know many of the details of the Master's life which in spite of my fairly long stay with him (running into many years) I was unable to learn, either from him or from anyone else. But how great was my surprise — not to say disappointment — when I found that I could not obtain even a glimpse of what my little mind was curious to know. Yet, after laying down the manuscripts and thinking about the matter for a while in the manner in which he has trained me to think, I realised the wisdom of his reticence. The one trait which is totally absent in him, and which he completely dislikes in anyone, is idle curiosity and profitless talk.

Sage Tiruvalluvar, who is justly regarded in the Tamil country as not merely a poet but also a lawgiver, has in his immortal poem, *Tirukkural,* devoted Chapter 20 in "Illaraviyal" (rules about householder's life), a section of "Arathuppal" (Dharma or code of conduct), to what is called "Payanila Sollamai" which means "non-utterance of what is fruitless." The truths which that poet expounds in the ten stanzas of that chapter are of inestimable value.

The eighth stanza says: "The wise who are competent to distinguish between what is useful and what is not will *never* give utterance to futile words."

xx

Sivananda's Studied Reticence

Swami Sivananda adopts this rule of conduct in his life and never, even in forgetfulness, swerves from it. He considers it wasteful to write about such incidents in his life as are not directly beneficial for the spiritual progress of the reader. That is the reason why we do not hear a word about why he left the shores of India and went to far-off Malaya in those days when orthodox Brahmin families regarded it a sacrilege to cross the seas. It is well known that Sivananda came from one of the most orthodox Brahmin families.

Again, what special circumstance made him give up a fairly lucrative job in Malaya and come back to our land bent upon pursuing the life of a Sannyasin? There are not a few disciples and admirers of his who wish to know whether he was a householder at any time and what happened to his family if he had one. Even the least curious among those who have the highest regard for his spiritual eminence are eager to know what he did in the Himalayas by way of Tapasya (austerity) and Sadhana (spiritual practices) of the conventional type which is generally undertaken by a novice; for it is their opinion that the pinnacle of spiritual excellence that he has reached is impossible of attainment without arduous and unremitting effort in the right direction. Even these earnest seekers are denied by our Gurudev the pleasure of knowing what he did to make himself the superman that he is.

It is undeniable that his studied reticence regarding these particulars is not due to any shyness in his nature, for where he speaks about himself he exercises no restraint upon his expressions. Perhaps, it is the other way. He often says things with an unparalleled boldness, unconcerned about the possibility of being regarded as boastful of his achievements. No, it is not shyness that has stood in the way. It is only his conviction that no useful purpose can be served by writing about them.

For instance, regarding the reason that prompted him to go to Malaya, suppose it was merely a spirit of adventure, a desire to see far-off lands: how are we as spiritual aspirants going to benefit by this knowledge? Suppose it was a feeling that he should serve the cause of the unfortunate Indian labourers who were in those days being practically decoyed by estate agents and their minions with promises of high wages and comfortable living but were actually subjected to considerable hardship. Even then, this knowledge will not help us to evolve into spiritual personalities. Knowing that a mention of this phase of his life will not prove useful to us, the author of this autobiography has not spoken a word about it.

Again, if there was a special circumstance which produced a radical change in his outlook upon life and made him eager to rush forth in all haste to become a Sannyasin, it is not necessary that everyone who has the urge to renounce the world should have the same experience that Sivananda had. When there is the irresistible divine call, anyone will be drawn automatically. Thus no useful purpose is served in mentioning the reason why the author renounced the world.

Clues to Sivananda's Sadhana

The same is the answer to the other questions,

including the Sadhana that he must have adopted. What one has to remember is that though books are written—and Swami Sivananda has also written many such treatises—about Sadhana with the object of instructing spiritual aspirants, the Sadhana which will be really effective, will be purely subjective and will relate to the particular individual himself and not to any other. All Sadhana is intended to make one's mind most helpful and least harmful. One's mind is one's own and not of anyone else. It reflects the consequences of one's actions in the past lives and in the present life. Each mind has to be handled in a special way and only the possessor of the particular mind will know from experience and practice that special way. Therefore, even if Swami Sivananda wrote elaborately about what obstacles he had to face in exercising control over his mind and how he faced them, it would be merely a bit of personal history and not anything which would help us in any way, however eager we may be to profit therefrom.

Yet, one cannot say that Sivananda has been completely silent in this matter. In the course of the autobiography, he has given us sufficient information here and there. He says: "The life of a mendicant during pilgrimages helped me to develop in a great measure forbearance, equal vision and a balanced mind in pleasure and pain. I met many Mahatmas and learnt wonderful lessons. On some days I had to go without food and walk mile after mile. With a smile I faced all hardships."

Surely this is a very brief account. But it is highly revelatory. It is not easy to walk mile after mile on an empty stomach and still preserve equanimity of temper.

That is real Sadhana. It elevates the individual more than a hundred *malas* of Japa sitting in a cosy corner without the pinchings of hunger. One can from such passages of the author understand the nature of the severe austerity that he must have undergone.

In another place he writes: "Self-realisation is a transcendental experience. You can march on the spiritual path only by placing implicit faith in the words of the sages who have realised the truth and have knowledge of the Self". These words are written in connection with his search for a Guru. Here we have an insight into the nature of his faith. It is by no means the faith of an ignorant person. He knew all the teachings about the Self that are in the *Upanishads.* Yet he fully recognized the need of a Guru. He knew that unless implicit faith is placed in the words of a Guru, the ego cannot be curbed. He teaches us this truth when he writes about his search for a Guru.

It is in this fashion that we have to learn about the Sadhana that he practised. The fact is that Swami Sivananda is a very practical person. What he learnt from books or men would be put into practice so that he might know how far the teaching suited him. If it did not suit him, he would not condemn it but merely shelve it. So far as he was concerned it was ineffective. That was all. So, whatever he writes about is experienced by him. He does not like torturing the body with the desire to attain spiritual powers and perform miracles. He writes about this too in this book.

Motive of the Autobiography

Sometimes a doubt arises in me as to whether a

saint should write an autobiography at all. Is there not, I ask myself, a tinge of vanity in writing about oneself and one's achievements? It may be pardonable for a worldly man to speak about himself in such a way as to obtain the good opinion of others. But is it right for a self-denying saint to do the same thing?

In answering this question, I find that Swami Sivananda is without any blame whatsoever because his book is only in name an autobiography. It does not contain anything which can be construed to have the motive of obtaining the respect and good opinion of the readers. He has had only one motive. He knows that though he did not plan anything, God had made him found the Divine Life Society, establish the Forest University (now known as Forest Academy), and do similar things all of which are at present satisfying the crying need of people all over the world: to live a life without fear and with faith in the protection of the Lord. He finds that whether he wanted it or not he is at the head of a great mission and, before he leaves the world, he would like to make people know how this noble movement can be used for the benefit of mankind. That is the main purpose, as I understand it, of his publishing this book with the title *Autobiography of Swami Sivananda*. Naturally the book cannot be compared with autobiographies of others which sprang from different motives.

Valuable Lessons in the Book

It is now possible to examine the value of the book. From the very beginning to the end, the book is of great educative value to the person who wishes to benefit himself. The great regard Sivananda has for his great ancestor, Appayya Dikshitar, is revealed in the opening chapter. Intentionally brief is his account of his parentage and boyhood. His love of the medical profession and the way in which ideal doctors are to do the job are revealed in his account of his Malayan career. How his faith in the injunction of the *Srutis* — "The day on which you get dispassion, renounce the world" — transformed him is seen in the section "Dawn of a New Vision." His life as a wandering mendicant, the benefits he derived from pilgrimages, his search for a Guru and his choice of Rishikesh for final stay are stated quite simply, without any embellishments of style. Yet they all have something to teach us. His observations upon the foolishly spiritually ambitious, his decision to adopt a synthesized Sadhana, the way in which he lived it at Swarg Ashram, the lecture tours and the journey to Kailas reveal his early attempts to combine Sadhana with service.

After this formative period in his spiritual evolution, we find him launching upon a career of mass disseminstion of spiritual knowledge. He has well described the different stages in which he started the Divine Life mission. Especially valuable are his remarks upon how his unselfishness and largeness of heart won for him the lasting attachment and devotion of his disciples.

The third stage — "The Birth of a Great Institution" — having been reached, he is happy in witnessing now the noble and invaluable work done therein. He then discovers himself as the cosmic friend and cosmic benefactor because he constantly lives in the spirit of the Upanishadic thought: "Aham Brahma Asmi — I am Brahman." He also engages himself in improving the natures of those who are by his side. What he does for them and with them is narrated in "Collective Sadhana" and the succeeding chapters. In due course the Divine Life movement gains strength and is found to meet the need of the hour because of the universality of its ideals and of the efficacy of its methods for spiritual perfection.

The author writes just as if he is writing an annual report, but the beauty of the book consists in the fact that the narration reveals in every sentence the nobility of his mind, the sincerity and seriousness with which he goes through his self-chosen task of benefiting mankind, and the love and respect with which he is regarded by his disciples, admirers and even casual visitors. In fact, it is the greatness of the man and his work that are seen through the unvarnished account of what actually happens in his Ashram. The rapid growth of the mission, which he states quite simply in a brief chapter, is proof to us that when a good man does something good, there is always God behind to help him. The chapters dealing with the nature of the Divine Life movement, which has no secret doctrines, which explains what true religion is, and which in reality is only a simple and practical way of living with ease and true happiness, are highly illuminating.

When we go on reading about the spiritual conferences, lecture tours, the organisations for Nagar Kirtan, Prabhat Pheri, etc., we see the dynamic work that has been done by Sivananda for ensuring that the maximum use is made of one's time to live up to the ideals of the Divine Life movement.

The author also gives us instructions about how

aspirants are to be cared for, how universal love should be practised and help rendered to all, and how disciples at a distance are to be looked after. The reproduction of some letters which he had written to his disciples reveals the great solicitude that he had for the spiritual and even material welfare of those who attached themselves to his service.

In the later part of the book, the author deals with many diverse matters such as the spirit of accommodation, glory of renunciation, need for renunciation even when one is young, the qualifications to be a good disciple, the need for the purification of the heart, the right attitude towards women, whether women can renounce the world, and many other topics of practical interest. Some of these chapters evidence his breadth of outlook and even a bold departure from time-honoured conventions, suited to the needs of modern times.

There is much valuable advice to Sannyasins about proper meditation, real service, about who can start Ashrams and who should not, about the relation between Sannyasins and politics, the value of initiation by a Guru, and other similar matters. The book, whatever its title, is a mine of most valuable advice and instructions.

Some chapters are devoted to the Master's books and other publications. There we find how he is very different from others, for he has no attachment for copyright. He has no commercial motive. He wants that, even after his passing away from the world, there must be a permanent stock of useful knowledge available to people in every part of the world. That is why he is a ceaseless writer. His books appear every year in increasing numbers and get distributed freely to thousands in India and elsewhere.

A part of the book deals with practical advice to his disciples not to quarrel, scandalise or even entertain thoughts of hate.

It is not possible to deal here with all the matters that are written about in this book. But this can safely be said: any page may be opened at random and there will be some teaching or other which will transform our inner nature. Every word that is written comes from the author's inner experience. He has, it is clear from the book, ever been at pains to keep his mind pure, exalted and noble, and been equally at pains to impart this same purity and nobility to his disciples.

Warning on Supernatural Powers

It is usual for the Master to warn us and also write in his books that a real spiritual aspirant ought not to hanker after Siddhis or supernatural powers because, when they are desired, further spiritual progress is arrested. He has seen some instances in which people who were making good progress were caught by the temptation to acquire these powers and from then on they had a serious fall. Nobody can dispute the correctness of the Master's opinion on this matter. But a doubt comes to me from time to time. Numerous are the letters received at the Ashram from people in different places mentioning many miracles performed by the Master. It cannot be that all who write such letters are uttering falsehood or are under any hallucination. It is likely that there is a small percentage of self-deceiving persons. But judging from the nature of the events reported to have happened — reported with many details and meticulous care in the narration — I have to come to the conclusion that the Master is exercising supernatural powers. If so, will he have a fall? I can safely assert that he cannot have a fall, because he has risen above the states of rising and falling. Since he has reached the stage in which he can identify himself with the Supreme — call It Atman or Satchidananda or Ishwara, as you like — where is the question of rising and falling? When the ego is negated how can there be any kind of danger?

Of one thing we can be certain: The real Siddha who does not want or care for Siddhis but who manifests them for unselfish reasons and as a result of communion with the Lord, is an entirely different person from the little man who has psychic powers to do things which are extraordinary or who has control over spirits. The power over spirits (good or bad) is entirely different from spiritual power. And no real Siddha goes about calling himself a Bhagavan or parading his powers. It can be said that the Siddha does not know that he performs miracles since they are not miracles to him — they are just ordinary things for him because he lives in the plane beyond the reach of the common man. I have to conclude that Swami Sivananda is one such. But he does not reveal himself as such to all and sundry.

Conclusion

Before concluding this introduction I cannot help stating that the author is — very probably unconsciously — revealing his real personality through

every sentence he has written. And what a grand personality it is! In this sense, this book is indeed a real autobiography.

We see in him, through his writings, that outstanding trait of his: the passion to help all — small and great, learned and unlearned — to realise, each in his own humble and limited way, that he is heir to the supreme bliss that pervades the entire universe, the bliss "from which all this (what we see as the world) has come, by which it is sustained and into which it merges." We see in him the unceasing endeavour to transform little natures into noble beings so that they may easily get over their different forms of bondage and live for ever in the eternal abode of bliss which is their birthright as the children of God.

PREFACE

(Sri N.C. Ghosh)

The Yoga-Vedanta Forest University, Shivanandanagar, has done India a signal service in giving us this fine autobiography of a great savant. Being an original product of Swamiji's genius, the book combines a searching analysis of his experiences with a depth of sincerity that at once carries conviction. The whole book is instinct with the prophetic vision of a seer, a man of Self-realisation, and the expression is so lucid and poetical that quite a new life has been breathed into the dry bones of philosophical discussion, and that too on the most abstruse subject ever known.

India's Spiritual Culture Enriched

Now the cultural heritage of India is glorified with the presentation of the inspiring life-story of Paramahamsa Swami Sivananda. It will do incalculable good to the whole world as it has in its characteristics many things unprecedented in other biographies. The Master's pen gives us an insight into his own personality, hints on practical spirituality, and an idea of the great spiritual heritage of India. It also provides us with a basis for universal understanding and sympathy, and a fascinating story of the foundation of the Divine Life Society, its subsequent development and the activities of this divine mission.

Amid the din and bustle of this atomic era, a spiritual

institution like the Divine Life Society is almost a paradox. Its expression of the infinite Spirit through a limited medium of philanthropic work and aesthetic culture is putting a stop to the downhill trend of many features of modern civilisation. It is not easy for the general public to have sufficient opportunities to get first-hand knowledge of the diverse activities of this institution and its illustrious Founder-President. In these circumstances this book will be found extremely handy and valuable. Within its short compass, the learned author has compressed much useful information on divine life and opened up a perspective that grips the attention of the reader to the end. He has described from his direct experience some incidents and events of his own life which are at once miraculous and instructive. Readers of a religious bent of mind all over the world will derive immense delight from the book, as it is a treasure of practical lessons for spiritual uplift.

The author brings out the essential features of India's spiritual culture for the common run of readers who, being steeped in worldliness but yet aspiring to walk the way of divine life, are unable or have no time to dive into the profundities of the great books like the *Vedas*. In a word, the book is a portrayal, however partial, of the Divinity whom the devotee should love and worship and cherish in his purified heart, and as such it is destined to awaken an aspiration for spiritual Sadhana in the reader.

An Ideal Personality

For the benefit of mankind Swamiji has tried to make the book helpful to all aspirants, giving a lot of information on the practical side of Sadhana. This autobiography gives a vivid picture of how his great heart bled for the suffering millions in India and abroad, and also what his plan was for the uplift of his motherland and the restoration of her past glory. If our young men wish to win the respect and admiration of the world let them draw inspiration from the wonderful life of Swami Sivanandaji, who is not only a seer and the greatest torch-bearer of Vedanta in the East, but the very personification of all that is great and noble in life. The magic personality of Swamiji, his vitality and endurance are wonderfully portrayed here. Written in chaste English and replete with soul-stirring incidents, this autobiography is sure to captivate the mind of the reader.

His novel and revolutionary methods of training his disciples which are depicted in this book shed a flood of light on our spiritual life also. Christ once said: "He that followeth me shall walk in darkness, but shall have the Light of life." The contemplative saint who has written this book throws light — well-focussed and going to manifold transformations — on the various aspects of Truth, which is unity. We are full of admiration for Swamiji. He is riding on the surging waves of popularity because the deepest truths of the profoundest philosophy have been so well blended with a stimulating story and written in such sweet and simple style that even the beginner can assimilate the lessons. The devotee, the Jnani, the Karma Yogi and others will immensely enjoy this book which is a mine of gold to introduce them to a new world of delight and ecstasy. They will have the one thing that is needful.

Sivananda — A World-Force

When Sivananda speaks, the world listens. His

resplendent personality and pristine perspective, brilliant intellect and all-compassionate disposition coupled with his impetuous fervour to uplift mankind have made him a veritable God-man.

Swamiji says: "To raise the fallen, to lead the blind, to share what I have with others, to bring solace to the afflicted, to cheer up the suffering, to love my neighbour as my own Self, to protect cows, animals, women and children — these are my aims and ideals. I will help you and guide you. I live to serve you all. I live to make you all happy. This body is meant for service."

This is his thrilling message to the people of this atomic age. Swamiji has, by years of arduous work, created a new world — "Ananda Kutir" or the "abode of bliss" — for the quick spiritual progress of all types of seekers after Truth, suitable to various tastes, temperaments and stages of evolution. Spiritual truth is eternal, but it has to be restated and redemonstrated in a human life in order that it may be a living and shining example before all of us. Swamiji's life is one of long stillness of prayer perfectly blended with dynamic activity through selfless service. The story is one of strenuous spiritual endeavour and service in the cause of suffering humanity, often in the face of great trials. The supreme devotion and efficient organising capacity of his worthy disciples on whom has descended the Grace of the Master have amazed everyone who has paid a visit to Swamiji's Ashram. It may be said without any hesitation that Swamiji's mission is well on its way to becoming a world-force.

The story of Paramahamsa Sivananda's life is a study

of religion in practice. Swamiji has astonished the world by the versatility of his genius, by the many-sidedness of his faculties and by the contributions, innumerable and diverse in character, which he has made to the world. Having attained realisation he has striven to impart the benefit of the citadel of Truth. The Siddha Jnanis, of whom there are great examples in human history, are personages like Lord Buddha, Jesus Christ, Ramakrishna Paramahamsa and others. Swami Sivananda himself, judging from the work he is doing, exemplifies the ideal type of Siddha Jnani.

Fulfilment of India's Spiritual Mission

It is the job of India to change the way of the world through her spirituality. India's true mission is to deliver her spiritual message to the world. The times need a change of heart. We wanted freedom because we thought that we had certain truths to preach, certain messages which were good not only for India, but for the whole world. India should achieve her true and noble mission by disseminating this message. In that mission, God-intoxicated men like Swami Sivananda are giving us the real lead. If India in bondage needed a Gandhi to lead her to freedom, resurgent India needs a Sivananda to make her conscious of her precious heritage and resume her spiritual mission.

Never was a man like him needed more urgently than today when the world, armed to the teeth with atomic weapons, hovers over the brink of a suicidal war. He is, as it were, a link between heaven and earth, and if anybody can contribute substantially to the peace and spiritual uplift of mankind, it is certainly Sivananda.

Even though there is poverty and misery in India, Indians are happy because they still have illustrious living saints like Swami Sivananda who in his clarion call asks us to seek the happiness of the soul and not material enjoyment. He is a saint of international outlook and is one of the pioneers who have brought the Yoga practices from the seclusion of the monastery within the reach of the common man. He is not lost in meditative contemplation to see the Unknown. He is a saint for the masses and has come down amongst us with a mission to show the truth in falsehood, to throw light on darkness and to establish immortality in this mortal world. In a word, he is the modern world prophet. Just go to the Sivananda Ashram and get a thorough physical, mental and spiritual overhaul—the picturesque Ashram in Rishikesh at the foot of the majestic Himalayas with the Ganga in the foreground and the Visvanath Mandir in the background, flanking the colony of saints who, under the divine leadership of Sadguru Sivananda Maharaj, live and work for the welfare of humanity.

Sivananda's Achievements

The Divine Life Society was established by His Holiness in 1936 and it exists today to serve mankind by the dissemination of spiritual knowledge and by training spiritual aspirants in Yoga and Vedanta in the Yoga-Vedanta Forest University. I humbly draw the attention of the world to this living saint and sage who is ever ready to extend his helping hand to every sincere seeker after Truth. His is a unique institution in that it is the great gift of a divine being who, paradoxically, combines in himself the cosmic consciousness of a sage, the dynamism of an enterprising industrialist, the daring of an adventurer, and a novel and refreshingly new approach to religious life. Therefore, it beautifully blends the essentials of the different ways of viewing and approaching God.

The two epoch-making events in Swami Sivanandaji's life are his All-India Ceylon Tour in 1950, and the Parliament of Religions convened by him in 1953. The warm reception that His Holiness received everywhere during his tour is not at all surprising. He held discourses at several universities and learned bodies, speaking mainly on universal peace and the message of Hindu philosophy. He won the respect of everyone who heard him because of his vast knowledge and his thought-provoking remarks.

A new chapter opened at Sivananda Ashram on April 3rd, 1953, a blessed day for India, when the Parliament of Religions was inaugurated. Indeed, it was for the first time in the history of this country that such a congregation of distinguished men and women from different parts of the world took place on the soil of India. This Parliament will, no doubt, be appraised by the world's philosophers and other intellectuals as one of the greatest achievements of the twentieth century.

Magnetic Influence of Sivananda's Life

Human language is an altogether inadequate vehicle to express supersensory perception. The reader will find mentioned in this work many visions and experiences that fall outside the ken of physical science and even psychology. With the development of modern knowledge the borderline between the natural and the supernatural is ever shifting. Genuine mystical experiences are not as suspect now as they were half a century ago. The words of Swami Sivananda have already exerted a tremendous influence in the land of his birth. Savants of Europe have found in his words the ring of universal truth. But these words are not the product of intellectual cogitation; they are rooted in direct experience. Hence, to students of religion, psychology and physical science, these experiences of the Master are of immense value for an understanding of religious phenomena in general.

In the spiritual firmament Swami Sivananda is a waxing crescent. He is a living embodiment of godliness and his message has spread across land and sea. There already exists a network of the branches of the Divine Life Society throughout India and abroad. Thousands have found solace in his teachings and experienced the miraculous powers of Swamiji ward off evils on their material and spiritual paths. The lofty ideals of peace and harmony which His Holiness exemplifies in his life have today become the watchwords of a world institution like the United Nations Organisation. He is being recognized as a compeer of Krishna, Buddha and Christ.

Service of humanity has been his one burning passion and this he has sought to fulfil by every means possible. The world-renowned Yoga-Vedanta Forest University has published over two hundred of his books on various subjects of absorbing interest but this book is their monumental epic, dwarfing all previous publications. It is indeed a true picture of Indian culture, tradition and dignity. In their breadth and depth they are unique. Great spiritual truths are here described in simple words and vivid stories, and the conflicts of religions are here solved in the light of direct experience. In those pages every man, whatever his religious creed, will find courage, faith, hope and illumination. Swamiji's life is a laboratory of religious experiment and his message is a silent force animating the national life of India. It is the precursor of a new age of light and understanding for the whole world.

Attracted by his irresistible spiritual power, hosts of people—men and women, young and old, educated and illiterate, agnostic and orthodox—have flocked to him. All have felt the radiation of his spirit and are uplifted in his presence. His love knows no barriers of race, colour or creed, and he gives without stint to all who seek him.

I am sure all pilgrims on earth will find the necessary "elixir divine" in the following pages at a time when it is so much needed in this materialism-ridden world. This book carries a message of inspiration for every day in the year and each message will leave a lasting impression on the reader's mind and may be a turning point in his life.

CONTENTS

Chapter Seven

LIGHT ON THE PATH OF RENUNCIATION

xliv

Chapter Eight

JNANA YAJNA

Chapter Nine

THE IDEAL OF LIFE

Chapter Ten

MY METHODOLOGY OF THE EVOLUTIONARY PROCESS

Chapter Eleven

PRACTICAL HINTS ON THE SPIRITUAL PATH

Chapter Twelve

SPIRITUAL EXPERIENCES

Chapter Thirteen

WISDOM IN HUMOUR

Autobiography of
SWAMI SIVANANDA

OM

CHAPTER ONE

I AM BORN

The Blessed Advent—Sri Dikshitar

On this blessed earth from which alone one can strive for and obtain Mukti, in which even Devas wish and have to be born for getting their final beatitude, appear, from time to time, some rare great Mahatmas, whose sole object of existence is to radiate love, light, joy and mercy all around, to serve the poor and the helpless, to bring solace to the forlorn and the depressed, to uplift the ignorant, to disseminate spiritual knowledge among the people and to bring unalloyed felicity and happiness to suffering humanity. These are the Saints and Sages, Arhats and Buddhas, Fakirs and Bhagavatas, Swamis and Yogins who have adorned this earth, at different times and in different climes. The Bhagavad Gita says:

"Having attained to the worlds of the pure doing and having dwelt there for immemorial years, he who fell from Yoga is reborn in a pure and blessed house. Or he may be born in a family of wise Yogins; but such a birth as that is most difficult to obtain in this world." (Chap. VI—41, 42)

Sri Appaya Dikshitar was one such. I have had the privilege to be born in such a great saint's family. Sri Appaya Dikshitar was born in Adaipalam near Arni, North Arcot District.

(3)

A Giant Among Geniuses

Sri Appaya Dikshitar, one of the greatest names in the annals of South India, is the reputed author of more than 104 works, embracing the various branches of knowledge in the Sanskrit language. The height of his intellectual eminence is evidenced by his works on Vedanta and all the Schools of Vedanta have drawn inspiration from his unique and unrivalled works. Of his Vedanta works, the 'Chaturmatasarasangraha' is justly famous for the scrupulous fairness with which he has expounded the tenets of the four great schools, Dvaita, Visishtadvaita, Sivaadvaita and Advaita, respectively in his 'Nyayamuktavali', 'Nyamayukhamalika', 'Nyayamanimala', and 'Nyayamanjari' (which together form the Chaturmatasarasangraha).

In almost all the branches of Sanskrit literature, poetry, rhetoric, philosophy, he was peerless not only among his contemporaries but even among scholars of several decades before and after him. 'Kuvalayananda' is generally regarded as one of the best works on rhetoric. His poems in praise of Siva are great favourites with worshippers of Siva. He has also written a learned commentary, entitled 'Parimala', on the Vedanta; it is a unique monument of philosophic erudition.

Sri Appaya Dikshitar's was a mighty intellect. Great is the reverence paid to him even now. He was equally revered in his own days. Once he went to a village, which was the birthplace of his wife. A grand reception was accorded to him by the villagers who were proud of calling him as one of themselves. There was a great excitement: "The Great Dikshitar is coming to us." The distinguished guest—Dikshitar—was greeted by crowds of people who flocked to have a sight of the great "Lion of Vedanta." An old dame, curious to a degree, came out, staff in hand, to see the "phenomenon." With the freedom that is conceded to her age, she made her way easily through the crowd and looked at Sri Appaya steadily for some minutes. Dim recollections of a known face floated in her mind. She mused I have seen this face somewhere and suddenly cried out, "Wait, O yes, are you not the husband of Achcha?" The great scholar confirmed her surmise with a smile. The good lady was disappointed; with her face and spirits fallen, she retraced her steps homewards remarking: "What ado they make, why it is only Achcha's husband!" Sri Appaya summarised a world of wisdom when he perpetuated the incident in a half verse—*'Asmin Grame Achcha Prasiddha'*—In this village name and precedence are Achcha's.

Great Spiritual Luminary

Sri Appaya is considered by many to be an Avatara of Lord Siva. When he went to Tirupati temple, in South India, the Vaishnavas refused him admission, as he was a Saiva. But, lo! In the morning the Vishnu Murti was found to have changed into the form of Siva. The Mahant was astounded and, begging Dikshitar's pardon, prayed to him to change the Murti again into Vishnu, which needless to say, the great saint did.

Sri Dikshitar lived in the middle of the 16th century. He was a great rival of Panditaraja Jagannatha in the field of poetry. He had no independent views on the doctrinal side of

Sankara-Vedanta but carried on fierce controversies with the followers of Vallabha at Jaypore and other places. His 'Siddhantalesha' is the most admirable digest of the doctrinal differences among the followers of Sankara. He was one among the greatest spiritual luminaries India has ever produced. Though a detailed account of his life-history is lacking, his works remain as sufficient testimony to his greatness.

My Birth-Place

Pattamadai is a lovely place with green paddy fields and mango groves all around; it is ten miles away from Tinnevelly Junction (in Tamil Nadu). A beautiful canal from Tambraparni known as Kanadiankal encircles Pattamadai like a garland just as Sarayu or Kaveri encircles Ayodhya or Srirangam. Tambraparni is known as Dakshina Ganga (Southern Ganga). As it passes through rocky beds which contain copper; it has the significant name, Tambraparni (*Tambra* means copper). The water is very sweet and health-giving. Pattamadai is famous as the place where the finest grass mats are made. People greatly admire the silk-like mat exhibited at the Sivananda Regalia.

My father Sri P.S. Vengu Iyer of Pattamadai, was descended from Sri Appaya Dikshitar. He was the Tahsildar of Ettiapuram Estate. He was a virtuous pure soul, a Siva-Bhakta and a Jnani. He was worshipped by the Rajah Sahib of Ettiapuram and the public at large. People used to say: "Vengu Iyer is a Mahan, a Maha Purusha." Justice Subramania Iyer was his classmate and had the greatest regard for him. He used to shed tears profuse— *Ananda-bhashpam*—whenever he uttered: "*Sivoham,*

Sivoham." His grandfather was a big Zamindar of Pattamadai. He was known as Pannai Subbier. Pannaiar means a landlord or Zamindar.

At Pattamadai there is an excellent High School, founded and then conducted by the erudite scholar, late Ramasesha Iyer, B.A., L.T. Another important feature of this place is that all children of the soil of Pattamadai have a good ear for music and can sing well. Pattamadai has produced many eminent musicians.

I was born to Srimati Parvati Ammal and P.S. Vengu Iyer, as their third son, on Thursday the 8th September, 1887, at the time of sunrise, when the Star Bharani was in ascendance. My elder brother, Sri P.V. Veeraraghava Iyer, was the personal assistant to the Rajah of Ettiapuram. My other brother, Sri P.V. Sivarama Iyer, was an Inspector of Post Offices. My uncle Appaya Sivam was a great Sanskrit Scholar. He was much revered by the people in Tinnevelly District. He has written many philosophical books in Sanskrit. Kuppuswamy was the name given to me by my parents.

In my youth I brought flowers and Bael leaves and prepared beautiful garlands and served my parents in their Siva Pooja.

The Budding Phase

Born in the family of devotees, saints and philosophers as a pet child, I was brought up carefully by my parents and received very good training. People used to admire my wonderful physique, well-developed chest and sinewy arms. The Rajah of Ettiapuram was all admiration for my well-developed body, my good manners and habits. I was bold, courageous, carefree and amiable by nature. In former days, especially in villages, there was no room for developing any evil habit at all. The environment and atmosphere were highly favourable for progress in education and culture. I was unusually active as a boy and had a highly pushing nature.

Even now I clearly remember, that when Lord Ampthill, the then Governor of Madras, came to Kurumalai Hills in 1901 for hunting, I was chosen to read the Welcome Address. I also sang a beautiful Welcome Song in English at the station platform of Kumarapuram, next to Koilpatti Railway Station. In the School Annual Prize Distribution, I used to get a lot of books as presents. Once I got the Globe Edition of Shakespeare and Macaulay's Speeches and Writings. I passed my Matriculation Examination in 1903 from the Rajah's High School, Ettiapuram. Then I joined the S.P.G. College, Trichinopoly, of which the Rev. H. Packenham Walsh was then Principal, who is now a Bishop.

I was interested in dramatic performances in the College. In 1905, when the Midsummer Night's Dream of Shakespeare was staged in the College, I played the part of Helena. I passed the Madurai Tamil Sangam examination creditably. I chose the medical course and ran a Medical Journal, *Ambrosia*, at Trichinopoly, for three years. I was very ambitious and enthusiastic.

I was a tremendously industrious boy in the school. During my studies at the Tanjore Medical Institute, I never used to go home in holidays. I would spend the entire period in the hospital. I had free

admission into the operation theatre. I would run about here and there and acquire knowledge of surgery which only a senior student would possess. An old Assistant Surgeon had to appear for a departmental test; he used to make me read his text books for him. This enabled me to compete with the senior students in theoretical proficiency. I was first in all subjects.

I had heard of an enterprising assistant in the Mannargudi Hospital. I wanted to become like him. With all humility I may mention that I possessed greater knowledge than many doctors with covetable degrees. At home my mother and brothers would persuade me to take up some work in some other line, but I was adamant in my resolve to stick to the medical line, as I had a great liking for it. All my leisure hours were spent in studying all kinds of medical books.

In the first year of my study in the Medical School I could answer papers which the final year student could not. I topped the class in all subjects. I studied Osler's medicine with Dr. Tirumudiswami in my first year. That was a rare privilege for me. Lt.-Col. Hazel Wright, I.M.S. loved me. Dr. Jnanam admired me as an ornament of the Institution. Even during holidays, I worked in the Hospital and learnt many new lessons.

I hit upon a plan that I should start a medical journal. I soon worked out the details. I got from my mother one hundred rupees for the initial expenses. I used to approach Ayurvedic physicians for articles on Ayurveda. I myself used to write articles on various themes and publish them in the "Ambrosia" under different pseudonyms.

The Magazine quickly gained popularity soon after its inception in 1909. Distinguished contributors started contributing for it. Once my mother wanted to celebrate some festival and was in need of about one hundred and fifty rupees to meet the expenses. I was ready with this sum.

The "Ambrosia" journal was successfully run for four years until I sailed for Malaya. It was of demi-quarto size, thirty-two pages each issue, and was quite beautifully got up. The material that its contents presented to the reader every month was attractive and highly useful to all medical practitioners. A significant spiritual touch could be felt in the pages of the "Ambrosia." Unlike other medical journals, the entire outlook was based on the teachings of the sages of yore. Spirituality was ingrained in me even in my youth.

Trials in Life

I was not satisfied with the running of the journal. I wanted to take up some job, with a view to maintain myself and to stabilise the journal. I, therefore, left Trichinopoly and went to Madras to join Dr. Haller's Pharmacy. Here I had to manage the accounts, dispense medicines and attend on the patients. Very hard work I had to do. I would finish all these, and yet find time to continue the editorial and circulation work of the "Ambrosia." I brought the old copies from Trichinopoly and despatched them to high officials and people of distinction in order to enlist their support. I resolved to seek a better position somewhere else. Finally, I decided to try my luck in the Straits Settlements of Malaya, and wrote to a friend, Dr. Iyengar who had his establishment next to

Dr. Haller sometime ago and later settled in Singapore. I wrote to Dr. Iyengar that I was planning to go to Malaya. I left Madras by S.S. "Tara."

I was unaccustomed to such long travels. I had no idea of the food I was to take on the way, of what preparations I was to make to begin my career in Malaya, and how much money was needed. I packed my things and did not forget to take a good consignment of sweets which my mother lovingly prepared for me. I belonged to an orthodox family and was frightened to take the non-vegetarian food on board the ship and so I carried a good quantity of sweets. In youth I liked immensely sweet preparations. Throughout the voyage, I managed to live with the sweets and drank plenty of water. Being unaccustomed to this diet, I reached Singapore almost half dead!

It was a bold adventurous bid to throw oneself on the high seas of uncertainty. I had no money to fall back upon in case of a reverse in my expectations. However, I had tremendous hopes and took a plunge to test the mettle of my destiny. Strength of will and a fiery determination played a lot in moulding my life and spiritual career. No easy-going prospect was awaiting me in the distant swamps of Malaya, as I was altogether unknown and friendless, with no financial safeguard whatsoever. I had to start from the very scratch and encounter disappointing setbacks in the beginning. But the later events turned out much in my favour and I felt my position secure.

Immediately after disembarking I went to the residence of Dr. Iyengar. He gave me a letter of introduction to an acquaintance of his, Dr. Harold

Parsons, a medical practitioner in Seremban, the capital of Negri Sembilan. When I reached Seremban, I found that Dr. Parsons was absent. By this time, the little money I had was spent away. I was highly optimistic about my getting a job. Dr. Parsons himself did not need an assistant. I was able to impress this physician in such a manner that he took me to Mr. A.G. Robins, the Manager of a nearby Rubber Estate which had its own hospital.

Fortunately for me, Mr. A.G. Robins was just then in need of an assistant to work in the Estate Hospital. He was a terrible man with a violent temper, a giant figure, tall and stout. He asked me: 'Can you manage a hospital all by yourself?' I replied: 'Yes. I can manage even three hospitals.' I was appointed at once. I had been told by a local Indian resident that I ought not to accept, in accordance with their policy, anything less than a hundred dollars a month. Mr. Robins agreed to give me one hundred and fifty dollars to start with.

The doctor who was in charge of the Estate Hospital had just then left. Moreover, I was told that he was not very competent. I quickly acquired a good knowledge of the hospital equipment and the stock of medicines, and found myself absorbed in the job. Here again hard work awaited me. I had to dispense medicines, in addition to keeping accounts and personally attending on patients as I did for Dr. Haller in Madras. Unusual handicaps began to tell upon me and I felt like resigning the job after some time, but Mr. A.G. Robins did not allow me to go.

Later on, when I was in Johore Medical Office, my assistants used to take too much advantage of my kindness and leniency and were super-lethargic in their duties. I had to do all their work as well. There I could not even complain of overwork lest my employer should be harsh towards them. The problem of my overwork was never solved in Malaya, still I continued in the same job.

I served in the Estate Hospital near Seremban for nearly seven years, after which I joined the Johore Medical Office, Ltd., at the instigation of Dr. Parsons who had by then returned from war service. I served in Johore for three years before renouncing the world.

In Malaya I came in direct contact with hundreds of the poor natives and indentured labourers as well as the local citizens. I learnt the Malaya language and conversed with the natives in their own tongue.

I served the workers of the estate nicely and endeared myself to them all. I gained the esteem of the employer and the employee alike. I was always fond of service. This moment I would be in the hospital; and the very next moment in some poor patient's house to attend on him and his family. Dr. Parsons who was a visiting physician to the estate hospital, loved me very much. I used to assist him in his private work also. Off and on I gave my earnings to help friends and the patients. I even went to the extent of pawning some of my own valuables.

I was a friend of both the management as well as the labourers. If the scavengers went on strike, the estate manager would come only to me. I would somehow run about here and there and bring them back to work. In addition to my own work, I would go about visiting other hospitals and acquire special knowledge in bacteriological and other subjects.

There was not a single available English medical book at that time that I had not read and digested. In addition to all this I would help my assistants too and train them for sometime daily, and then send them to other hospitals with a recommendation letter, providing from my pocket their railway fare as well as some emergency money. Soon I became well-known in Seremban and Johore Bahru. The Bank Manager would oblige me at any time even on holidays, by honouring my cheques. I became everybody's friend through my sociable disposition and service. I got rapid promotions and with that my salary and private practice increased by leaps and bounds. All this was not achieved in a single day. It meant very hard work, unflagging tenacity, strenuous effort and indomitable faith in the principles of goodness and virtue and their practical application in my daily life.

During my career in Malaya, I contributed many articles on 'Public Health' to "Malaya Tribune," Singapore.

First Lessons in Service to Humanity

I specialised in microscopical study and Tropical Medicine. Subsequently I moved to Johore Bahru, near Singapore, to join Drs. Parsons and Green and lived there for three years. Doctors Parsons, Green, Garlik and Glenny complimented me as highly competent for the medical profession and admired me for my agile, nimble and efficient nature. I was happy, cheerful and contented. I carefully attended on all patients. I never demanded fee from my clients. I felt happy when they were free from disease and trouble. To serve people and to share what I have is my inborn nature.

I used to cheer up people with my wit and humour, and elevate the sick with loving and encouraging words. The sick persons at once felt a new health, hope, spirit, vigour and vitality. Everywhere people declared that I had a special gift from God for the miraculous cure effected in the patients and acclaimed me as a very kind and sympathetic doctor with a charming and majestic personality. In serious cases I used to keep vigil at night. In the company of the sick, I understood their feelings and endeavoured to relieve their sufferings.

I became a Member of the Royal Institute of Public Health (M.R.I.P.H.), London, a Member of the Royal Asiatic Society (M.R.A.S.), London, and an Associate of Royal Sanitary Institute (A.R.San.I.), London. During my stay in Malaya, I published some medical books such as "Household Remedies," "Fruits and Health," "Diseases and their Tamil Terms," "Obstetric Ready-Reckoner," "Fourteen Lectures on Public Health." I gave shelter to many people during their days of unemployment and gave them food and clothing and fixed them up in one office or another.

I was liberal in my views. The spirit of Sannyasa was ingrained in me. Crookedness, diplomacy, double-dealing, are not known to me. I was very candid, straightforward, simple and open-hearted. I trained many young persons in the Hospital where I worked and fixed them up in various Estate Hospitals. I spent all my energy and time in relieving human sufferings by serving the poor and the sick, day and night, with a sympathetic heart. This kind of selfless service gave me purification of heart and mind, and led me to the spiritual path.

In my youth I had a great liking for high class dress, collection of curious and fancy articles of gold, silver and sandalwood. Sometimes I used to purchase various kinds of gold rings and necklaces and wear them all at a time. When I entered shops, I never used to waste any time in selection. I gathered all that I saw. I did not like haggling and bargaining. I paid the shopkeepers' bills without any scrutiny. Even now, whenever I enter a book-shop, I purchase a lot of books and add them to the Forest University Library for the benefit of the students in the Ashram.

I had many hats, but never wore them. Sometimes I used my felt cap and the Silk Turban like a Rajput Prince. I prepared my own food for a long period. Biking was my best exercise. I entertained guests and served them with great love and devotion. Malaya was a land of temptation, but nothing could tempt me. I was as pure as a crystal and did my daily worship, prayers, study of scriptures. I used to conduct Nandan Charitram and played on Harmonium and sang Bhajans and Kirtans. Even in Malaya I practised Anahat Laya Yoga and Svara Sadhana.

CHAPTER TWO

THE CALL OF THE IMMORTAL

Dawn of a New Vision

"Is there not a higher mission in life than the daily round of official duties, eating and drinking? Is there not any higher form of eternal happiness than these transitory and illusory pleasures? How uncertain is life here? How insecure is existence on this earth-plane, with various kinds of diseases, anxieties, worries, fear and disappointments! The world of names and forms is constantly changing. Time is fleeting. All hopes of happiness in this world terminate in pain, despair and sorrow."

Such were the thoughts constantly rising in my mind. The doctor's profession gave me ample evidence of the sufferings of this world. For a Vairagi who has a sympathetic heart, the world is full of pain. True and lasting happiness cannot be found merely in gathering wealth. With the purification of heart through selfless service, I had a new vision. I was deeply convinced that there must be a place—a sweet home of pristine glory and purity and divine splendour —where absolute security, perfect peace and lasting happiness can be had through Self-realisation.

I frequently remembered the Sruti Vakya: "*Yadahareva Virajet Tadahareva Pravrajet*—The day on which one gets Vairagya, that very day one should renounce the world." I constantly thought of: "*Sravanartham Sannyasam Kuryat*—For hearing the

Srutis, one should take Sannyasa." The words of scriptures have great value. I gave up the life of ease, comfort and luxury, and reached India in search of an ideal centre for purposes of prayer and contemplation, study and a higher form of service to the whole world.

In 1923, I renounced the life of ease and money-making and took to the life of a mendicant, a true seeker after Truth. I left my luggage in Malaya with a friend. A School Master in Malaya who came to the Ashram in 1939 told me: "Mr. S. is still keeping all your articles intact, awaiting your return!"

As a Wandering Mendicant

From Singapore, I reached Banaras and had Darshan of Lord Siva. Then I proceeded to Nasik, Poona and other important religious centres. From Poona I walked to Pandarpore, a distance of seventy miles. On my way I stayed for a couple of days in the Ashram of Yogi Narayan Maharaj at Khedgaon. Then I spent some four months in Dhalaj on the banks of Chandrabhaga. During my incessant travels, I learnt how to adjust and adapt myself to various types of people.

I learnt a lot from the lives of Yogins, Mahatmas and great men. The spirit of service ingrained in me enabled me to lead a smooth life of peace everywhere. The life of a mendicant during pilgrimage helped me to develop in a great measure Titiksha (forbearance), equal vision and a balanced state of mind in pleasure and pain. I met many Mahatmas and learnt wonderful lessons. On some days I had to go without food and walk mile after mile. With a smile, I faced all hardships.

How to Benefit by Pilgrimage

Mahatmas and devotees go on pilgrimage and visit sacred places as a part of spiritual Sadhana. They have different objects in view. Mahatmas come in contact with sincere devotees at various centres and impart their knowledge and experiences, and guide them. They select suitable places for meditation where they find inspiration and facility for intense Sadhana. They clear the doubts of the householders, give their blessings and guide them. Devotees who take to pilgrimage get Darshan of Mahatmas and have their doubts cleared. They receive inspiration by seeing holy men and sacred places and develop various kinds of divine qualities by mixing with various types of people. They are trained to adopt a simple living and bear hardships.

There are some who spend their entire life in pilgrimage by wandering frequently from Kadirkamam (in Ceylon) to Mount Kailas (in Tibet), Puri to Dwaraka, Amarnath (in Kashmir) to Allahabad, Banaras to Rameswaram. I have seen many persons repenting in old age that they had so wasted their youth in such a wandering life. I led the life of a wandering monk, just for a short period, in search of my Guru and of a suitable place charged with spiritual vibrations, for spending my life in seclusion and to do rigorous Sadhana.

Necessity of a Guru

The spiritual path is beset with many obstacles. The Guru will guide the aspirants safely and remove all sorts of difficulties they have to face. He will inspire the students and give them spiritual powers through his blessings. Guru, Isvara, Truth and Mantra are one. There is no other way of overcoming the vicious worldly Samskaras of the passionate nature of raw, worldly-minded persons than personal contact with and service to the Guru.

In search of a Guru, I reached Rishikesh and prayed to the Lord for His Grace. There are many egoistic students who say: "I need no Guru. God is my Guru." They change their own robes and live independently. When difficulties and troubles confront them, they are bewildered. I do not like the rules and regulations of the scriptures, sages and saints to be violated. When there is a change of heart, there should be a change in the external form also. The glory and the liberty of a Sannyasi can hardly be imagined by the timid and the weak. From the sacred hands of Paramahamsa Viswananda Saraswati, I received Holy initiation on the bank of the Ganga on 1st June, 1924. The religious rite of Viraja Homa was done for me by my Acharya Guru, Sri Swami Vishnudevanandaji Maharaj at Kailas Ashram.

A personal Guru is necessary in the beginning. He alone can show you the path to attain God, who is the Guru of Gurus, and obviate the snares and pitfalls on your path. Self-realisation is a transcendental experience. You can march in the spiritual path only by placing implicit faith in the words of sages who have realised the Truth (Apta Vakya) and attained knowledge of the Self.

Guru's Grace is needed by the disciple. This does not mean that the disciple should sit idle and expect a miracle from the Guru to push him directly into Samadhi. The Guru cannot do Sadhana for the student. It is foolish to expect spiritual attainments from a drop of Kamandalu water from the Guru. The Guru can guide the student, clear his doubts, pave the way, remove the snares, pitfalls and obstacles and throw light on the path. But it is the disciple himself who has to walk every step in the spiritual path.

Spiritual progress requires intense and unswerving faith in the teachings of the Guru and the Sastras, burning and lasting Vairagya, yearning for liberation, adamantine will, fiery resolve, iron determination, unruffled patience, leech-like tenacity, clock-like regularity, child-like simplicity.

If you have no Guru, take Lord Krishna or Siva or Rama or Christ as your Guru. Pray to Him. Meditate on Him. Sing His Name. He will send you a suitable Guru.

The Journey's End

I came to Rishikesh in June 1924 and found it my destination. My Guru gave me initiation and enough spiritual strength and blessings. Gurus can do this much only. It is the student who has to do intense and rigorous Sadhana. Rishikesh is a Railway Station in the District of Dehra Dun, Uttar Pradesh, in the Himalayas. It is a holy place with many Mahatmas. There are Kshetras (alms-houses) to provide free food for all Sadhus and Yogins and aspirants. They can stay in any of the Dharmasalas or Kutias or have their own thatched cottages and huts in any place. Near about Rishikesh, there are many charming places like Brahmapuri Forests, Nilakantha, Vasishtha Guha, Tapovanam. Sadhus who stay in such places get their dry rations once in fifteen days and prepare their own food.

The scenery of the Himalayas is charming, soul-elevating. The Holy Ganga is a blessing. One can spend hours in contemplation, sitting on a rock or on a sand-bank by the side of the Ganga. There are some Libraries from where we can get authoritative works in Sanskrit, English and Hindi on Yoga and Philosophy. Some learned Mahatmas conduct regular daily classes and give private tuition to deserving students. The climate of the place is fine—slightly cold in winter (November to March) and slightly hot in summer (April to June). There are allopathic and Ayurvedic Hospitals to attend to the sick. Thus I found Rishikesh an ideal place for intense and undisturbed spiritual practices true for all seekers after Truth.

CHAPTER THREE

ON THE ANVIL—SHARING THE TREASURE DIVINE

Vagaries of Spiritual Ambitions

Some Mahatmas spend their whole life in deep study of scriptures and derive great pleasure in hot discussions and arguments on abstruse points of Yoga and Vedanta. Some Yogins struggle with Hatha Yoga exercises with the hope of getting Siddhis. They indulge in practices which torture the body. There are a few who are tempted by the Kundalini Yoga and Tantra Sastra for attaining spiritual powers to perform miracles. Devotees spend all their time in Japa and Kirtan and weep for hours because of their separation from the Lord. In this group, you will find also some educated young persons who spend their whole time in writing thrilling articles and lectures. They plan and prepare for a world-tour. I have great love and reverence for all such Mahatmas for the thorough research they do in various directions. Do they all succeed in attaining perfection?

I found that they did not have proper facilities, comforts and conveniences. They lacked guidance from a competent person. They could not be steady and systematic in their Sadhana. The planning and scheming nature in them led them to frequent changes in their daily practices. Either they paid undue attention to their wants or completely ignored their health. They all thought much of the future and aspired for Siddhis, miracles, name and fame. That only fattened their ego. A deep study of the ways of Mahatmas opened my eyes and gave me strength to stick to rigorous Sadhana in the right direction. I felt the Grace of the Lord. I derived strength and guidance from within. I found ways for an all-round development. I had the goal of my life as Self-realisation and determined to spend every bit of my energy and time in study, service and Sadhana.

How I Synthesised My Sadhana

Service of the sick and the poor and the Mahatmas purifies the heart. This is a field for developing all divine qualities such as compassion, sympathy, mercy, generosity. That helps to destroy the evil qualities and impurities of the mind such as egoism, selfishness, pride, hatred, anger, lust, jealousy, etc. Mahatmas and the poor villagers who were sick did not have proper medical aid. Thousands of pilgrims to Badrinath, Kedarnath also needed medical help. Therefore I started a small dispensary, *Satyasevashram*, at Lakshmanjhula on the way to Badri-Kedar, and served the devotees with great love and devotion. I arranged special diet for the serious cases and provided milk and other requirements. Spiritual evolution is quicker through service done with proper Bhav and attitude.

For maintaining a high standard of health, I practised Asanas, Pranayamas, Mudras and Bandhas. I used to go out for long brisk walks in the evenings. I combined physical exercises such as Dand and Bhaitak also. I paid special attention to simple living, high thinking, light food, deep study, silent meditation and regular prayers. I loved

seclusion and observed Mauna. I did not like company and futile talk. From the Ram Ashram Library in Muni-ki-reti I used to get some books for my study and devoted some time to study every day. I kept always a Dictionary by my side and looked up the meaning of difficult words. Rest and relaxation gave me enough strength to carry on intense Sadhana. I moved closely with some Mahatmas but I never indulged in discussion and debates. Self-analysis and introspection were my guide.

With a view to devoting more time to prayer and meditation, I moved to the Swargashram. I lived in a small Kutir, 8 feet by 10 feet, with a small verandah in front, and depended on the Kali Kambliwala Kshetra for my food. Now the Kutir is numbered as 111 with some additional rooms by its side. I continued my Sadhana and service to the sick persons of the place. Just for an hour daily, I used to go from Kutir to Kutir to attend to the sick Mahatmas, enquire about their welfare and supply their requirements. I spent much of my time in meditation and practised various kinds of Yogas in my Sadhana, and my experiences have all come out in many of my publications as advice to aspirants. I quickly sent out my thoughts and experiences to help the world and struggling seekers after Truth. It was usual for even great Mahatmas to keep their rare knowledge as a secret and teach only a chosen few.

Life at Swargashram

I did not spend much time in cleaning the teeth, washing clothes and bathing. I quickly finished these when I was a bit free from my Sadhana, study and service. I never depended on any one though there were a few disciples who were awaiting opportunities to serve me. I had fixed times for all items of work such as study, writing notes and letters to Sadhakas, exercises, going out for Bhiksha, etc. Gradually people came to me in large numbers. That seriously affected my systematic work. With the permission of the Kshetra people, I fixed up a barbed-wire fencing around my Kutir and locked the gate.

Before the visitors, I did not show my erudition by discussing high philosophy at length. I gave some short hints on practical Sadhana and disposed of each of them in five minutes. I kept a sign board at the entrance of my compound: "INTERVIEW— between 4 and 5 p.m.—only for five minutes at a time." During winter, the devotees were not many. I utilised this time for a brisk walk in the compound, singing Bhajans and songs. For some days, I would not come out of my Kutir. For my food, I used to keep some dry bread, remnants from my daily alms. Thus intense Sadhana was my Goal.

My joy was indescribable when I spent hours in the evenings on the sand banks of the Ganga or sitting on a fine rock and gazed at wonderful Nature. I became one with Nature. During this period, I established the Swargashram Sadhu Sangha, to obtain redress for the grievances of the Mahatmas, and registered the Institution. I invited great Mahatmas and organised weekly discourses and daily Bhajan and Ramayana Katha for some time. For some months, we had discourses on the Yoga-Vasishtha, Tulasidas Ramayana and Upanishads also. I trained my students in organisational work through the Swargashram Sadhu Sangha.

Out on Divine Ministration

In 1925 I visited Sherkot Estate, Dhampur, in the District of Bijnoor. The Rani of Sherkot, Srimati Phulkumari Devi, gave me a cordial reception. I conducted Bhajan there on several days and gave medical aid to the villagers. The Maharani of Mandi, Sri Lalita Kumari Devi, also attended the Bhajan. Whenever the Maharani met me, even after several years, she used to say: "I cannot forget your melodious, inspiring songs. They are ever green in my memory. I can now feel their influence. They lulled me and elevated my soul."

From Sherkot I returned to Rishikesh by walk after visiting the villages on the way. I gave discourses on Yoga and conducted Kirtans and Bhajans to the groups of devotees I met. Occasional tours helped me to develop all divine qualities and to serve mankind on a large scale. Once during my Parivrajaka life, I visited Rameswaram and saw the sacred places in South India. At this period I stayed in Sri Ramana Ashram for some time. Sri Chand Narain Harkuli, Advocate, Sitapur, accompanied me. On my way I went to Puri and worshipped the Lord Jagannath. I took bath in the sea at Waltair. At Rameswaram I worshipped Lord Ramalinga. I reached the Ashram on the day of Sri Ramana's Birthday celebration. I did Bhajan and Kirtan in the big Hall before Sri Bhagavan Ramana and the devotees and perambulated the Arunachala Hill and worshipped the Tejas Linga.

Whenever I found an opportunity to serve people

on a large scale or when people compelled me to preside over Spiritual Conferences, I visited various centres in Bihar, Punjab and United Provinces. I started dynamic centres for Sadhana and organised Spiritual Conferences and Kirtan Sammelans and participated in the activities of many educational, religious and spiritual Institutions. Even while travelling in trains I taught Yoga exercises to the passengers and gave them simple lessons on Japa and meditation. I carried a chest of medicine with me always and gave medical aid to the sick.

The important places of my visit were; Lahore, Meerut, Srinagar (Kashmir), Patna, Monghyr, Lucknow, Gaya, Calcutta, Ayodhya, Lakhimpur-kheri, Bhagalpur, Ambala, Aligarh, Sitapur, Bulandshaher, Delhi, Shikohabad, Nimsar, Mathura, Brindavan, Etawah, Mainpuri and many other places in Northern India. In Andhra Province, I visited the Santi Ashram in Totapalli Hills, the Mission of Peace in Waltair and also went to Rajahmundry, Kakinada, Pithapuram and Lakshmi-narasapuram.

During my travels, I carried a bundle containing my ink-pot, pens, pencils, pins, study books like Viveka Chudamani, the Upanishads, the Gita and the Brahma-sutras. I kept also some postage stamps to attend to some urgent correspondence work. I used to go to the Railway Station two hours before the scheduled train timings. Instead of looking here and there, I would sit under a tree and attend to my writing work. I never kept any address book with me for meeting devotees or friends at important centres of my travel with a view to getting nice food or financial help. I quickly finished my work for which I was travelling and returned to Rishikesh by the first available opportunity.

I visited Kedarnath and Badrinath, Tunganath and Triyuginath. Swami Balananda, Swami Vidyasagar accompanied me. I had a dip in the hot-water springs at Badri Narayan. Throughout my travel I sang Kirtan and Bhajan and did mental Japa.

By a steam-boat at Calcutta, I reached Ganga Sagar—the confluence of Ganga with Bay of Bengal. Srimati Maharani Surat Kumari Devi also was with me. There is a small temple of Kapila Muni at the sacred Ganga Sagar. I had a bath in the sea. There was a Mela (fair). I helped the pilgrims in getting up the ladder.

Call of Mount Kailas

In the early years of my Sadhana at Rishikesh, I decided to see Kailas. Mount Kailas is in Western Tibet. On the 12th June, 1931, I started on a pilgrimage to that sacred place with His Holiness Sri Swami Adwaitanandaji, Sri Swami Swayam Jyoti Maharaj, Sri Brahmachari Yogananda, Her Highness Maharani Sahiba Surat Kumari Devi, O.B.E., Singhahi State, and Sri Kedarnath, her secretary. We all had a dip in Lake Manasarovar and went around Mount Kailas. I walked the whole distance. There is no place on all this fair earth which can be compared with Kailas for the marvellous beauty of the everlasting snows. Of all Yatras, the Kailas trip is the most difficult. It is called Mount Meru—the axis of Mountains. At the time I went there, His Highness the Maharajah Saheb of Mysore also visited Kailas. He is the only Maharajah in India who has visited the sacred mount. The total distance from Almora to Kailas is about 230 miles. In two months one can easily visit the place and return. On August 22nd our party returned to Almora.

Mass Dissemination of Spiritual Knowledge

On the 9th September, 1950, I started on a dynamic Mission of Dissemination of Knowledge, undertaking an extensive tour all over India and Ceylon for a period of two months. I returned to Rishikesh on the 7th November, 1950. I then came in close touch with thousands of sincere spiritual aspirants all over the land. I rejoice heartily that the Almighty gave me an opportunity to serve Him and His children by undertaking the All-India-Ceylon Tour. I recollect with immense delight the deep devotion of the people of India and Ceylon, the reverence they have for the Holy Order of Sannyasa and their eagerness to acquire the Knowledge of Yoga and Vedanta.

I visited all the important cities, towns and villages all over India. I addressed public meetings and conducted Kirtans. I delivered speeches in many Schools, Colleges and Universities on ethical culture and Real Education and addressed numerous public meetings on general spiritual topics. Several thousands of rupees worth of valuable books were distributed free of cost to the public during this historic event—the All-India-Ceylon Tour.

In keeping with my usual practice, I did not spend any time in preparing fine lengthy speeches on Yoga, Bhakti and Vedanta for such occasions. Along with my Kirtans and songs, I gave practical lessons on

Sadhana. That created a wonderful effect on the audience. When I was filled with immense joy in the company of devotees, I combined Nritya also—the Dance of Lord Siva and Lord Krishna. People were thrilled. Even today thousands repeat my favourite Kirtans: "Agada Bhum," "Chidananda-hum," "Pilade," etc. In various centres, the devotees also stood up and danced for a long period in divine ecstasy.

Everywhere I went, I was overwhelmed by the love of the people. I enjoyed at every centre the warmth of the people's cordiality and devotion. I bathed again and again in the ocean of the masses' devotion to the Lord. I drank again and again the Immortal Elixir of the Lord's Name, which all people sang with Bhava and fervour.

Service gives me Joy. I cannot live without service even for a second. I found a dynamic field in the All-India Tour. I worked without any rest or relaxation for a period of two months. I felt that the Tourist Car and the scheduled timings for the travel by Aeroplane, Train, Cars and Steamers imposed a restriction on my method of Intense work. I had to stick to 'time' in attending to various functions and did not have enough time to attend to the needs of the devotees.

When I was at Bombay on my return journey, I wanted to dispense with the Tourist Car at Delhi and then to continue the tour from Province to Province, going from door to door in every city, town and village and singing Kirtans and Bhajans and repeating Maha-mrityunjaya Mantra for the health and long life of the devotees. I wanted to carry the Message of Divine Life to each and every aspirant individually.

Spiritual Conferences

Though I had a special predilection for deep meditation in seclusion during my stay in Swargashram, periodically I organised Satsangas in the evening hours. I invited the Mahatmas and the Brahmacharis. One Punjabi Mahatma used to conduct classes on the Yoga-Vasishtha and Tulasidas Ramayana and before closing I did Bhajan and Kirtan. Occasionally I visited Sitapur, Lakhimpur-kheri, Meerut and other places in the U.P. and Punjab. I conducted Kirtans at night, lectures in all High Schools and Colleges with demonstration of Yoga exercises and distributed leaflets on "Twenty Important Spiritual Instructions" and "Importance of Brahmacharya." I introduced common prayers and silent meditation in the early morning at 4 a.m. and compelled all the devotees to join the collective Sadhana.

I asked people to maintain Likhita-Japa (writing of Mantras). I saw many devotees sit in public meetings motionless, write Mantras and observe Mauna during the period. I distributed presents to those who wrote the largest number of Mantras legibly. To encourage people, I gave spiritual books as presents not only to the winners in the competition but also to every one present in the Hall. Devotees used to bring a lot of fruits, and the entire lot used to be distributed to the audience then and there. At the end I used to take a small bit as Prasad.

Lecture Tours

Invariably the organisers used to chalk out a tight programme for a week or two. There used to be

Akhanda Kirtan for 2 or 3 days. To relieve me in the work at out-stations, I used to take my students, Sri Swami Svarupananda and Sri Swami Atmananda. The former would quickly and ably translate my English speeches into Hindi and the latter conduct melodious Bhajans and Kirtans. Many pamphlets and leaflets were printed for free distribution.

In 1933 I took up this propaganda tour in Lakhimpur-kheri, Meerut and Hardoi. Every year, for a week or two I travelled in the Punjab and in Bihar. During such tours I asked my students In Swargashram and the Post Master at Rishikesh not to redirect my letters. I did not attend to this correspondence work during my tour and concentrated on a dynamic work for dissemination of knowledge.

Though I lived a simple life with ordinary dry bread (Rottis) at Rishikesh, during such intense work, day and night, I felt the need for energy-giving food and fruits. I used to keep a few pieces of bread or biscuits in my pocket, because the work in various places did not allow me any time for my meals or rest. Before starting for such Conferences, I kept enough money with me for my return fare. For my expenses I never demanded money from the organisers of the functions, but I asked them to print a large number of copies of leaflets and pamphlets in different languages for wide circulation during the Conference or Sammelans.

My students who accompanied me in the tours invariably said: "It is all joy to travel with Guru Maharaj for the wonderful treatment he gives." I shared with them all that I had and took great care of their health and made them very popular and well-known. Sometimes I wrote to the organisers: Keep enough fruits and biscuits in my room. That is my Saguna Brahman. To bring about a solid and substantial work, the workers need nutritious food and energy-giving fruits." In Sitapur during my visit in 1934, I started a Medical Relief Campaign. In Andhra Districts, during my tour, I visited many villages and gave medicine to the poor village people. Sri Swami Omkarji and Sister Sushila (Sri Ellan St. Clair Nowald) accompanied me.

Unfailing Inspiration

During intense work, I used to relax through Japa, meditation, deep breathing exercises, Bhastrika Pranayama, and Kirtan; and that energised and galvanised me. I conducted Nagar Kirtans and Prabhat Pheri in many places. The whole town, wherever I went, was charged with spiritual vibrations. People felt the wonderful peace and power for days. Devotees used to write to me after several years: "Beloved Swamiji, we hear your OM chanting and Maha-Mantra Kirtans even today." People who work in the fields even now repeat my popular Kirtans: "Om Namah Sivaya, Chidananda-hum, and Sita Ram Sita Ram," Dhwanis. The students in all Colleges and Schools repeat my favourite Kirtan: "Govinda, Govinda—Don't smoke, Govinda." The results of the tour were wonderful and lasting.

The work at the Ashram was heavy and I gave up the tour life in 1938. To various centres I sent my students to attend the Spiritual Conferences at out-stations. People from Punjab compelled me on various occasions and did Satyagraha (strike) at my

Kutir and forced me to visit Lahore during their Annual Sankirtan Conferences in December.

Dynamic Transformation of the Masses

Some of the letters written by me from 1933 to 1936, reproduced below, give an idea of the work turned out during my travels:

I. "When I travel, I pour out all my energy in the course of a week. I am tired now. But people compel me to visit Meerut. It is all His Grace. May His Will be done. Do not send any letters to my camps. It will interfere with my work here. People are devouring me from all corners. Nothing is definite. I may return to Rishikesh after one or two weeks."

II. "My time is spent in delivering thrilling lectures during day and Kirtans at night. I pump joy and power into the devotees. I roar like a lion. People do not leave me even a second. Sitapur and Lakhimpur-kheri are Vaikuntha now on earth. I had a Virat Kirtan with 3000 people, a thing which Lakhimpur has never seen in its annals. I will have Kirtans with Harijans today. Through Kirtan Movement, we can revolutionise India. India needs this. There is a great revival now."

III. "Tell the organisers that I am slightly pleased with them now. Akhanda Kirtan for 3 days on a separate platform is very, very necessary. This is the only effective part of the work, solid and substantial. Sankirtan in different centres to thrill and electrify the whole atmosphere is another task. These two items are important for the peace of the world. Local riot and Section 144 are nothing before Ram Nam. You need not be afraid of the curfew orders."

Types of Different Kirtans

Even today I can easily visualise how, when I sang Agada-Bhum Kirtans, thousands used to get up and dance. After every Bhajan and Kirtan, I gave impressive lessons on Sadhana. I conducted Lorry Kirtans in Bihar. I went to various places in a Lorry with a party of devotees and did Kirtans. In Rishikesh, on several occasions, I did Boat Kirtans.

Another highly interesting feature was the Group Kirtans. I selected the Government officers from the audience for doing Kirtan from the platform. Then a chance was given to all College Professors, doctors, students, ladies and girls. That created great enthusiasm. It was a novel feature. At first they all hesitated and felt shy. Then they felt the benefit. After some months they all turned to be staunch Kirtanists and established Kirtan Mandalis in various towns.

CHAPTER FOUR

THE DIVINE MISSION
First Stage

How Students Are Trained

I always loved silent Sadhana in seclusion. During the day for a short period I would write some articles and letters to thirsty aspirants. I did not use a kerosene light, nor did I work at night at any time. I used to come out of my Kutir just for an hour in the morning to serve the sick people with medicine, for a brisk walk in the compound, to bathe in the Ganga and to go to the Kshetra for bringing my food. This sort of routine has become my habit during my thirty-five years of life in Rishikesh. I never indulged in loose talks with friends. When I went to the Kshetra, I observed Mauna. To avoid people, I used to walk through a small foot-path through the jungle. While walking to the Kshetra, I combined deep breathing exercises and mental Japa.

I had no ambition to become world-famous by any extensive tour or thrilling lectures from the platform. I never attempted to be a Guru to anyone. I am not pleased when people call me: "Sat Guru" or "Avatar." I am dead against "Gurudom." That is a great obstacle and has caused the downfall of great men in the spiritual path. "Gurudom" is a menace to society. Even now I ask people to do Namaskar to me mentally. The few lines I wrote to one of my disciples in 1931 convey my attitude clearly:—

"I am only a common Sadhu. I may not be able to help you much. Further I do not make disciples. I can be your sincere friend till the end of my life. I do not like to keep persons by my side for a long time. I give lessons for a couple of months and ask my students to meditate in some solitary places in Kashmir or Uttarkashi."

Reserve and Humility

I never said or did anything to tempt people with promises of grand results like Mukti from a drop of Kamandalu water or Samadhi by a mere touch. I emphasised the importance of silent Sadhana, Japa and meditation for a systematic progress in the spiritual path. Invariably I asked all aspirants to purify the heart through selfless service to mankind.

In 1933 the publishers in Madras wrote articles on my life and mentioned me as an "Avatar." Immediately I gave a reply which explains the attitude I have always maintained:—

"Kindly remove all 'Krishna Avatara' and 'Bhagawan' business. Keep the publication natural and simple. Then it will be attractive. Do not exaggerate much about me very often. The juice will evaporate. Do not give me titles as 'World Teacher', 'Mandaleshwar' and 'Bhagawan'. Lay bare the truth, Truth will shine, I lead a simple and natural life. I take immense delight in service. Service has elevated me. Service has purified me. This body is meant for service. I live to serve everyone and make the world happy and cheerful."

Even before donkeys and other animals, I do mental prostrations. To my disciples and devotees, I

first do Namaskara. I behold the Essence behind all
names and forms. That is real Vedanta in daily life.

Guiding the Steps of Neophytes

From 1930, many earnest students with a burning
desire to devote their lives to spiritual pursuits came
to me for guidance. I had also a burning desire to
serve the world. Those were the days when Sadhus
and Mahatmas lived in peculiar, pitiable conditions—
without necessary comforts and conveniences and
proper guidance for spiritual evolution. Many tortured
the body in the hot sun and in the Himalayan cold.
Some were addicted to intoxicating drinks to induce
the so-called Samadhi.

With a view to training a band of Sannyasins and
Yogins on the right lines, I permitted some aspirants
to live in the adjacent Kutirs. I arranged for their meals
from the Kshetra and gave them initiation. I arranged
all comforts and conveniences for them. I encouraged
them and infused Vairagya in them. I took special care
of their health. I frequently enquired about their
Sadhana and gave useful hints for the removal of
their difficulties and obstacles in their meditation.
When they offered their services to me, I asked them
to go from Kutir to Kutir and find out the old and sick
Mahatmas and serve them with Bhakti and Sraddha
by bringing food for them from the Kshetra and
massaging their legs and washing their clothes.

I asked some educated students to take copies of
my short articles and send them to magazines and
Newspapers for publication, and devote their time to
study, Japa and meditation. They all took great
pleasure in copying out my articles, as they all

contained the essence of the teachings of all sages and saints, and a clear commentary on the difficult portions of the Upanishads and the Gita. My articles contained practical lessons for controlling the turbulent senses and fluctuation of the mind.

Instead of studying the ancient sacred scriptures for decades, the students spent a few minutes daily in making copies of my articles and thereby learnt Yoga and philosophy easily in a short period. I closely observed their faces to see if they liked the work and then carefully selected matter suited to their taste and temperament and entrusted them with the work. Sometimes I had to do the whole work. I love the students. Unasked, I attended to their needs.

In the case of old persons who had no ties in the world, I welcomed them and encouraged them in carrying on their Sadhana and asked them to take bath in the Ganga and do plenty of Japa and Sravana. I danced in joy when I saw peace and bliss in their face. Thus more and more aspirants came to me, and the Swargashram management could not maintain the increasing number of seekers after Truth. I loved the place and enjoyed the peace, but in the interest of the spiritual uplift of a large number of educated Sadhakas, I decided to leave the Swargashram.

Second Stage

Planting of the Acorn Sapling

Planning and scheming were not in my nature. I depend on the grace of the Lord. I had decided to leave Swargashram. Where was I to go? That was a great problem. For some days, I stayed in a small

room at the Rama Ashram Library. A few of my
students lived in a small Dharmashala nearby and
depended on the Kshetra for their meals. For some
days I too went to the Kshetra for my Bhiksha. To
save time, I received my Bhiksha through an elderly
Sadhu from the Kshetra. Thus months passed.

Then I found a small Kutir in a dilapidated
condition nearby. That was improved a bit by fixing
doors and windows. I occupied the place and lived
there for a period of over 8 years. I could have easily
set up some thatched cottages in the jungle. That was
not suitable for dynamic work. Books and papers
might get damaged by white-ants. I saw a series of
rooms in a Dharmashala used by a shopkeeper as a
cow-shed. These rooms had no doors. Gradually, one
by one, all the rooms were converted into residential
quarters for the students.

When devotees gave me some money for my
personal use, I utilised it in printing leaflets like
"Twenty Important Spiritual Instructions," "Way to
Peace and Bliss," "Forty Golden Precepts" and other
pamphlets, and gave them to visitors. I utilised the
money in purchasing some useful medicines for the
treatment of sick Mahatmas and for postage to send
articles to newspapers and letters to thirsty aspirants.
The work grew in a steady pace. I did not go out in
search of students.

True seekers of Truth came to me in large
numbers seeking my help and guidance. They all
received initiation from me and lived in the adjacent
rooms of the Dharmashala and worked day and night.
To meet the heavy rush of work, I got a duplicator and
a typewriter. People evinced great interest in the

divine service done for the spiritual uplift of the world. I admired their devotion to me. In work, they forgot their past and plunged themselves in attaining evolution through service and Sadhana. Devotees gave me voluntary contributions for the noble cause. For the maintenance of the students, I received dry rations for five persons from the Kali-kambliwala Kshetra at Rishikesh. For the rest of the students and the visitors I utilised the meagre donation received from a few admirers. That enabled me to publish some books also for sale.

Talents Find Their Best Uses

With the arrival of new and able hands, I started various fields of activities suited to their taste and temperament. I found out the talents and hidden faculties in them and encouraged them to a great extent. Then a small kitchen was started to provide food for the hard workers, the visitors and the helpless who could not get Bhiksha from the Kshetra. I maintained various kinds of addresses—of devotees, High Schools, Libraries, donors and aspirants for the Sannyasa line (Nivritti Marga) and sent my books periodically for dissemination of knowledge. The addresses were well-classified under several headings for easy reference. Here I give the titles of a few address books:

Ashrams, Associations, Advocates, Judges, Graduates, Book-sellers, Publishers, Firms, Doctors, Correspondence students, Divine Life Society Branches, Libraries, Ladies Section, Brahmacharis and Sannyasi students, Magazines and Periodicals, Maharajahs and Zamindars, Students who have received initiation, Monthly Donors, Household

Disciples, Officers, Patrons, Professors, Wonderful Misers. Now there are several address books, a separate volume for each country. I myself used to fill in the correct addresses and note the changes very carefully. Even today, I myself enter the important addresses and permit the students to maintain all the address books in perfect order.

Third Stage

Birth of a Great Institution

Systematically to carry on the Divine Mission on a large scale, I established the DIVINE LIFE TRUST SOCIETY in 1936 and registered the Trust Deed at Ambala. In 1936 when I was returning from Lahore after prociding over a Kirtan Conference, I just thought of a Trust Society and alighted at Ambala and consulted an Advocate and prepared the Trust deed. Then the Divine Life Society was established for the dissemination of spiritual knowledge throughout the world and subsequently about 300 Branches were opened in all important cities. Thousands of students received initiation from me into the order of Sannyasa. So long as they undergo training they stay with me and work. Advanced students start their own Mission in big cities or have their own Sadhana in the Himalayan caves.

Thirsty aspirants in all parts of the world receive guidance through post. Series of articles come out on the practical side of Yoga, Bhakti, Vedanta and Health through leaflets, pamphlets and bigger publications, in various languages. Leading newspapers in all countries publish my articles on Yoga, Health and general spiritual matters. Half a dozen periodicals are published at the Ashram in English and Hindi for circulation through the world. The Ashram is now in a position to maintain about 400 persons, learned and cultured scholars, Mahatmas, Yogins, devotees, poor people and the sick, not to mention the school students of the neighbouring villages.

A Centre of Dynamic Spiritual Regeneration

Many foreigners come to the Ashram and spend some weeks or months and admire the wonderful work turned out at the Ashram. The inhabitants of Shivanandanagar, young and old, men and women, enjoy the peace and bliss of this Holy Centre and help the world in a variety of ways. They all receive my careful, personal attention. I provide them with all comforts and conveniences and help them in their evolution.

There are a number of buildings, Kutirs and Guest Houses for their stay. Over thirty typewriters work day and night for attending to correspondence and book-work. The Yoga-Vedanta Forest University trains a large number of students through able and qualified professors and teachers. The students become well-versed in all the scriptures. The University Press is now equipped with several electrically operated automatic machines of composing, printing, folding and binding. For the dissemination of knowledge among youths, Essay Competitions are conducted and scholarships offered to prosecute their studies in Colleges and High Schools.

The Sivananda Hospital is a blessing to the Mahatmas, Yogins, pilgrims and the poor people of the neighbouring villages. Experienced doctors in different systems of medicine attend to the Hospital work. The General Hospital is equipped with modern apparatus like X-Ray, Diathermy and a High Frequency Apparatus for E.N.T. and eye cases.

Special worship in the Lord Viswanath Mandir has given a new life to the sick persons all over the world. People get peace and prosperity by such worship done in the name of the devotees. I am filled with immense joy when I receive hundreds of letters from devotees who say that their lives were saved through the special prayers conducted in the Temple of all Faiths at the Ashram. They write volumes on the miraculous escapes they had in their lives.

Leaders and followers of other religions and cults also come and stay at the Ashram and find this an ideal centre—a common platform—to serve the world. I see before me a huge Spiritual Colony with Joy and Bliss in the face of every resident. People come with many motives (such as attaining material and spiritual benefits) and they are all stunned to have their wishes fulfilled in a large measure. Glory to the Lord for bestowing this Ideal Centre for all types of seekers after Truth.

In addition to the normal activities, occasional Blind Relief Camps are organised at the Ashram and at out-stations also. Provincial Divine Life Conferences are organised in important cities of India. Devotees and students come in batches during their holidays and join the daily routine and Satsanga, and derive incalculable spiritual benefits.

Fourth Stage

Collective Sadhana

Young aspirants, because of old habit, used to sleep in the winter cold till sunrise or till 6 or 7 in the morning. They must not waste their precious life in sleeping in the Brahmamuhurta, between 4 and 6 in the early morning. That period is highly favourable for deep meditation. The atmosphere also is charged with Sattvic vibrations. Without much effort one can have wonderful concentration at this period.

From my Kutir, I used to chant aloud several times the Mantras: "OM OM OM, SHYAM SHYAM SHYAM, RADHESHYAM RADHESHYAM RADHESHYM" and thus made my students get up early for prayers and meditation. This had no effect on the Tamasic type of aspirants. I arranged their night meals before sunset. That enabled some to get up early morning. It is only those who load the stomach heavily at night that find it difficult to get up early in the morning.

In the beginning stages of Sadhana, even if people meditate alone in a room, they get up in the morning only to see that they were overpowered by sleep, and sleep the whole period in a sitting posture. This gave me an idea of a common prayer and meditation during Brahmamuhurta. One student would ring the bell in front of every Kutir and collect the aspirants in a common place for the collective Sadhana. I joined the group daily for some months and years.

Prayer and Study Classes

The function started with prayers to Lord Ganesha, Guru Stotra and Mahamantra Kirtans. One student would read a Chapter of the Gita and explain the meaning of one Sloka. Another student gave some short hints on concentration and meditation. In the end, I spoke for half an hour on attaining quick spiritual progress and suggested various methods for destroying the evil tendencies of the mind and controlling the turbulent senses. I laid great emphasis on ethical perfection. The function came to an end with the chanting of ten Santi Mantras in chorus. The students kept up the divine consciousness even during their work in the day.

Some students lived in Brahmananda Ashram, a furlong away from my Kutir. On many occasions I paid surprise visits to the Kutirs at 4 a.m., and chanted OM several times and made them get up for prayers. I did not compel all the students to join the common meditation. I permitted them to have their own Sadhana in their own Kutirs. Thus I paid all my attention to the spiritual uplift of my students. Even now many students who attended in those days the common prayer and meditation say how they were inspired by my short speeches on Sadhana.

In the evening also I organised a "Study Class" between 3 and 4. I asked one student to read a Chapter from any of my books. On the next day I used to put questions on the important points. I trained the aspirants in a variety of ways. They all specialised in chanting the Mantras of the scriptures, conducting Kirtans, delivering short lectures. I asked one student to put questions and others to answer them. In the evening class, I introduced Likhita-Japa and in the early morning, Trataka and other Yoga exercises. During the day, they should all prepare essays on Yoga and philosophy and write about their own experiences. Even today when school boys and young children come to the Ashram, I teach them a few short sentences in English and ask them to deliver a powerful lecture. Many have learnt my English Kirtans, like "Eat a little."

I trained my students in organisational work, typing, maintaining proper accounts managing the affairs of the Society and in attending to the devotees, visitors and the sick. Thus even in the early stages, the Yoga-Vedanta Forest University was vigorously in its working.

Attention to Visitors

When visitors came to me, instead of talking to them on their family affairs, I asked them to forget the past and sing Kirtans with me. I taught them music, Bhajan, Kirtan and philosophy. Even today when devotees come to the Ashram, I prescribe a book for their study and on the next day, I ask them questions. I clear all their doubts and give helpful suggestions for the removal of their troubles and obstacles.

They all feel happy in receiving my personal attention. The systematic work done at this sacred centre in the Himalayas on the banks of the Ganga, attracted thousands of seekers after Truth from all distant places in India and other countries. The Divine Life Society, the Yoga-Vedanta Forest University and the Sivananda Ashram became "watch-words" for all aspirants. Similar work is now organised systematically in various centres with the formation of Branches of the University, The Divine Life Society, Sivananda Ashram and Sivananda School of Yoga.

I pay much attention to the diet of the aspirants at the Ashram. Here they have enough to keep themselves quite fit—not for luxury or craving of the senses, but helpful items for progressing in Sadhana.

I introduced saltless diet on Sundays, simple boiled potatoes and bread on Ekadasi days or only milk and fruits for some students. I started the work with a dozen students.

In a short period, a large number of devotees came to me during holidays from Delhi, Madras, Calcutta and other cities in India. Then I introduced a Collective Sadhana—a special programme with the important items of Sadhana—a kind of Spiritual Conference on the practical side of Yoga. This took the shape of Sadhana Weeks during Easter and Christmas holidays. And now this has become a regular feature during the last twenty years.

Various Branches of the Divine Life Society in India organised similar Conferences with the routine of the Sadhana Week at the Ashram. They invite great men to deliver lectures during these Conferences. They print several leaflets, pamphlets and books for free distribution on the occasion. Thus there is a dynamic work for spiritual awakening all over the world.

CHAPTER FIVE

MY RELIGION, ITS TECHNIQUE AND DISSEMINATION

The Divine Life Movement

I love seclusion. I have to hide myself at times. I do not crave for name and fame. I did not spend much time in a deep study of all the scriptures and religions of the world, for preparing thrilling lectures. I never liked to spend time in writing fine essays for publication through books or newspapers. I was not pleased when people called me: "Mahatma, Guru Maharaj." I never planned for any Institution to perpetuate my name. But the Divine Will was different. The whole world came to me with all divine glory and splendour. That may be due to the intense prayers of thousands of sincere seekers after Truth coupled with my own inborn tendencies to share with others what I have and to serve the world on a large scale on the right lines, for the attainment of Light, Peace, Knowledge and Power.

I was induced to start the Divine Life Society when I found some facility and useful hands to carry on the work. I carried the Message of the Sages and Saints and taught the world the way for Peace and Bliss. Because of the popularity of the Divine Life Society, many learned and pious souls from far off lands have come to see me and, sharing with me the love for selfless service, are doing valuable work in spreading right knowledge, which alone can confer lasting peace and happiness. Many foreign Branches of the Divine Life Society are reprinting parts of my writings and distributing them free in their respective regions.

The Need of the Hour

When man gets entangled in selfishness, greed, lust, passion, he naturally forgets all about God. He always thinks of his body, family and children. He constantly attends to his food, drink, comforts and conveniences. He is drowned in the ocean of Samsara. Materialism and scepticism reign supreme. He gets irritated by little things and begins to fight. There is restlessness, misery, panic and chaos everywhere. Now the whole world seems to be in the grip of materialism. The invention of new kinds of bombs causes terror everywhere. People have lost faith in holy scriptures and the teachings of the sages and saints. People have become irreligious owing to wrong education and evil influences.

The stirring events since the advent of the twentieth century did not fail to have their effect upon all spiritual-minded people, Sannyasins, saints and men-of-God. The horrors of world wars moved them greatly. The fateful epidemic and the world-wide depression that followed it, touched their compassionate heart. They saw that the sufferings of mankind were mostly brought on by its own deeds. To awaken man to his errors and follies and to make him mend his ways so that he may enthusiastically utilise his life for attaining worthier ends, was felt to be the urgent need of the age.

Millions were eagerly looking for such guidance. This silent prayer was heard and I saw the birth of the

Divine Life Mission with its task of rescuing man from the forces of bestiality and brutality and divinising his life upon this planet.

Just at this critical juncture, I started the Divine Life Society. Now people consider it a blessing to the world. It has as its basis the quintessence of the teachings of all religions and of all saints and prophets of the world. Its principles are broad, universal, all-embracing and in accordance with science and reason. It has set for itself the task of raising man above the sorrows and miseries of this mundane life by making him see the Blissful Divinity that is hidden behind all outward forms.

Good thoughts pervade and influence all good people. The thought-currents generated by the Divine Life Movement have had their effect upon the people of Europe and America, and now there is a great thirst for peace all over the world. Millions dread the speedy termination of the race by nuclear weapons.

Universal Ideals for Spiritual Perfection

The Divine Life Society is an all-embracing and all-inclusive Institution; its objects, ideals and aims are very broad and universal. It does not condemn any of the principles or tenets of any cult. It includes all the fundamental principles of all religions and cults. There are no pet dogmas or sectarian tenets. It leads people to the spiritual path. It enables people to take easily to the Divine Life even while living in the world and following the teachings of some particular cult or religion.

The Society has brought about a vigorous awakening throughout the world and has contributed much to a new life of freedom in action, a life of harmony amidst worldly turmoils and a life of bliss through mental non-attachment and mental renunciation of desires, egoism and mine-ness. There is universal appreciation of the principles, aims, ideals of the society and the method of its work. It lays great stress on the practical side of Sadhana. It expounds in a rational and scientific manner the Yoga of Synthesis. Members belonging to various institutions and organisations in all parts of the world become members of the Divine Life Society and write to me for spiritual guidance. I take special care of them and give them lessons through post for their spiritual progress and welfare. The Divine Life Society proclaims that any man can attain Wisdom in his own station of life, be he a Brahmachari, Grihastha, Vanaprastha or Sannyasi, be he a scavenger, Brahmin, Sudra or Kshatriya, be he a busy man of the world or a silent Sadhaka of the Himalayas. Divine Knowledge is not the sole property of Sannyasins, recluses.

It explains how although the central basis is Jnana Yoga, Vedanta, it is necessary for one to practise Karma Yoga for purification of mind and heart; Hatha Yoga to keep up good health and strength and purify the Prana and steady the mind; Raja Yoga to destroy the Sankalpas and induce concentration in meditation; and Jnana Yoga to remove the veil of ignorance and ultimately rest in one's own Satchidananda Svarupa.

The Critical Juncture

Students became irreligious,
They lost faith in religion,
Under the influence of Science,

They neglected Dharma,
They began to smoke and gamble,
Girls became fashionable,
Officers became materialists,
Health of people deteriorated,
People shunned the scriptures,
Materialism had its sway.

At this critical juncture,
To revive the Glory of the Lord,
To disseminate knowledge of Yoga,
To preach the Yoga of synthesis,
To instil devotion and faith in people,
To work for the spiritual uplift of mankind,
To bring peace and bliss to every home,
I established the Divine Life Mission,
And founded the Yoga-Vedanta Forest University,
In a sacred, charming spot in the Himalayas,
On the banks of the Holy Ganga in Rishikesh.

Rapid Growth of the Mission

I started the Divine Life Society in 1936 for the spiritual uplift of mankind. I trained many sincere students in Yoga. For their quick spiritual evolution, I introduced the morning common prayer classes with Group Asana Class. To the local poor people and thousands of pilgrims I gave medical aid by starting a free dispensary. Experts were sent to various centres to deliver lectures on Bhakti, Yoga and Vedanta. A small temple was erected for prayers and worship. When a large number of students came for training, boarding and lodging facilities had to be provided for all the students and visitors; and thus Sivananda Ashram came into being.

The Yoga Vedanta Forest University came into existence when regular classes began to be conducted on all Branches of Yoga. To help the students all over the world, the University Press was established for printing necessary works on the practical side and half a dozen periodicals, with a number of machines to do the work automatically. The small dispensary grew into a big Sivananda Medical Organisation, with a General Hospital and a building of its own. Though the Divine Life Society continues to be the Central organisation, to fulfil the various functions that have developed to carry out organised work, many other institutions had to come into existence. Now the Ashram, a very big Spiritual Colony, looks like a huge factory with the wonderful, indescribable Peace of the Himalayas. Spiritual aspirants who come to the Ashram and stay there for months or for years, find that there is scope for spiritual progress both as workers in the different institutions of the Ashram and as silent meditators in the temple precincts or in the jungle retreats of the neighbourhood, and each chooses his line according to his own bent of mind.

Basic Approach

More than to strive to reach a Heaven after this life, the followers of the Divine Life try to make conditions of Heaven prevail upon earth. The tenets of the Divine Life Society are perfectly non-sectarian and universally applicable. The basis of this Movement is adherence to the triple ideal of truth, non-violence and purity—the common fundamental tenets of all the religions throughout the world. Therefore the Divine Life Movement has the willing cooperation of the peoples of all faiths and cultures, a Plan of Life and a Goal that is common and acceptable to all upon earth, who wish to rise above sorrow and obtain lasting Bliss. This, then, is the Divine Life Movement.

No Secret Doctrines

The Path of Divine Life Sadhana is no other than the essence of all Yogas and the main essentials of all religions. Here everyone finds the features suitable and unoffending to his own faith or belief. The great need for a vigorous and intense working of its Ideals is more than ever patent today, because the most recent developments in the fields of science, politics and sociology have tended to bring mankind nearer than ever to the brink of the dangerous precipice of total agnosticism and violent self-destruction. Hatred and violence, untruth and deceit, vice and impurity are fast becoming the order of the day.

A strong counter-force alone can possibly balance to some extent this downward trend. Thus to counteract these baneful influences that are rampant today and to check man's whirling rush towards ruin, the Divine Life Society was established. I carry the message of peace, goodwill, spiritual fraternity and the realisation of the oneness of Spirit. There are neither petty dogmas nor secret doctrines nor esoteric sections in this Divine Life Movement. Lovers of Truth realise its fullness, infinite beauty, majesty and splendour. It gives room and shelter for all. It enables one to realise the religion of the heart, the religion of oneness.

What Is True Religion

Not by mere argument or discussion can religion

be taught. Not by precepts or moral canons alone can you convert a person to be religious. Not by pointing to your loads of sacred literature or the miracles of your Chief can an aspirant be won over. Practise religion and live upto its teachings if you want to evolve and attain the Goal of Life. Whatever be your religion, whosoever your prophet, whichever be your language and country, whatever be your age or sex, you can easily grow if you know the way to crush the ego, to destroy the lower nature of the mind and to have mastery over your body, senses and mind. This is what I have found out to be the way for real Peace and bliss eternal. Therefor I do not try to convince people by heated debates and arguments.

Real Religion is the Religion of the heart. The heart must be purified first. Truth, love and purity are the basis of real religion. Conquest of the lower nature of man, control of mind, cultivation of virtues, service of humanity, goodwill, fellowship and mutual amity, constitute the fundamentals of true religion. These ideals are included in the mottoes of the Divine Life Society. I am very particular in propagating these ideals on a wide scale.

I do not waste time in finding out suitable authoritative statements from scriptures to satisfy the curiosity of aspirants. I lead a practical life and try to be an example to the students for moulding their lives. Know that true religion begins when you go above body-consciousness. The essence of the teachings of all sages and saints, the fundamentals of all religions and cults, are the same. People needlessly fight over non-essentials and miss the Goal.

May the Divine Life Movement, the harbinger of

peace, harmony and exalted life shed its lustre and glory throughout the world!

Gospel of Divine Life

The world of unreality is beset with many difficulties at every step that we take to attain the Goal—Nirvana—which the Lord Buddha attained after years of determined and steady struggle. The modern thinker has neither the requisite time nor the patience to perform rigorous Tapas and austere religious practices; and some of these are even being relegated to the superstitious level. In order to give the present generation the benefit that will result from religious practices, to reveal to them their real significance and also to convince them thoroughly of their efficacy and usefulness, I taught my gospel of DIVINE LIFE, which is a system of religious life suited to one and all, which could be practised by the common office-goer as well as the obscure labourer without undue interference in the performance of their daily round of duties. The beauty in "Divine Life" is its simplicity and practical applicability to everyday affairs of the ordinary man. While following the teachings of his own religion, a man can attain quick spiritual evolution by following the principles of Divine Life.

Practical Aspect

The average seeker after Truth is often deceived by the caprices of his mind. A person who takes to the spiritual path is bewildered before he reaches the end of his journey, and is naturally tempted to relax his efforts half-way. Many are the pitfalls, but those who plod on steadily by leading a Divine Life are sure to reach the goal of their religious aspiration, i.e.,

Self-realisation. I have laid great emphasis in all my writings upon disciplining of the turbulent senses, conquest of mind, purification of heart, attainment of inner peace and spiritual strength, to suit the different stages of evolution, the taste and temperament of each individual.

Role of Divine Life Branches and Spiritual Aspirants

My message to individual spiritual aspirants and to the Branches of the Divine Life Society is as follows:

"You have come to this earth to attain spiritual perfection. You have come here to attain supreme and unalloyed Bliss. The purpose of human birth is the achievement of Divine Consciousness. The Goal of life is Self-realisation. Man is not a sensual animal. Man, in his essential nature, is an ever free, ever pure, ever perfect, immortal, spiritual being. Feel that you are the Immortal Self. You are Satchidananda. Remember 'Ajo nityah sasvatoyam puranah,'—you are unborn, eternal, imperishable and ancient. To live in this exalted Consciousness is to experience indescribable joy every moment of your life, to experience a limitless freedom in the Spirit. This is your birthright. This is the aim of your life. This is the goal. To realise this through a life of truth, purity, service and devotion is the chief purpose of the Divine Life Movement.

"Fear dominates in this era of nuclear weapons of mass destruction. Hatred rules the policies of vast sections of the so-called enlightened and civilised mankind. This age of advancement has been exposed to be in reality an age of degeneracy in the views and values, the ideals and morals of the greater masses of mankind. At this juncture, cultured men and women all over the world look to the sacred land, India, for light and knowledge. It is your noble task to spread this light of spiritual knowledge and spiritual Idealism to all corners of the globe."

Oneness of Humanity

"The Upanishads say: 'All this is verily the Atman. The One, blissful Self indwells all beings.' The spiritual oneness of all humanity is a great lesson man needs today. Whatever has been and whatever will be in the future, all this is verily the one, eternal Being alone. The Message of Divine Life is: 'See God in all faces. Serve all. Love all. Be kind to all. Be compassionate. Feel everyone to be your own. Serve your fellow beings in the spirit of worship offered to the Divine which indwells them. Service of man is truly the worship of God.' Let this message ring freedom from end to end in every land. Let this message enter into every home and into the heart of everyone.

"All great religions of the world do verily declare this divine message of the spiritual basis of man's life. They do verily declare the universal brotherhood of man under the fatherhood of the Almighty Lord. Know well that the heart of the Vedas, the heart of the Bible, the holy Koran, the sacred Gathas and all the world scriptures are in truth one and sing in unison the sweet message of love and concord, goodness and kindness, service and worship. Discard the barriers of name and form. Seek the oneness at the heart of all beings. Include within your spiritual embrace entire humanity. Live for peace. Live for universal love. Live in the Life Divine."

The Clarion Call of Divine Life

"A Divine Life Branch is a great blessing to man in the present age. It is a veritable boon from the Divine. It is a field of dynamic Yoga, a field of practical Vedanta. Spread of Divine Life is the hope of mankind. Through Divine Life shall man free himself from ignorance, pain and suffering and go beyond sorrow into the realms of peace and bliss now and here, in this very life. Divine Life brings peace and brotherhood to mankind. It purifies man, ennobles his nature and unfolds his glorious, hidden, divine personality. Divine Life is the gift of India to the world at large.

"Let the clarion call of the Upanishads ring through every village, town and city. Let the glorious chant of divine Name fill all quarters. Let virtue be implanted in every heart and Dharma and the good life be seen in every walk of life. Divine Life must be practical. Ideals of Divine Life must shoot up into practical realisation. Divine Life must be made vigorously manifest in the lives of the people. This is important. Be sincere. Work with concord. Be adaptable. Adjust, adapt and accommodate. Remember always that work is the important thing, not personal views and individual opinions. Therefore dissolve all differences and work together for the cause of a pure life and spiritual perfection.

"Perfection of the individual leads to the perfection of mankind ultimately. Spread the doctrine of selfless service. Inspire all to follow the path of Yoga and attain the Goal of life, fine health and long life." It is not through rules and regulations and restrictions that I tried to help the seekers after Truth. Stage by stage,

I gave instructions through letters, periodicals and valuable publications to all the students for creating some spiritual vibrations through collective prayers, common meditation, Bhajans and Kirtans. For spiritual progress, it is not number that counts. Even a single sincere student can move the world and bring light and knowledge to the world.

The following letters written to my students between 1936 and 1940 will clearly explain how I started a dynamic campaign all over the world and established over 300 Branches of the Divine Life Society.

(1) Importance of Collective Sadhana

"Evolution is quicker through collective Sadhana, mass prayers and common meditation. The purpose of Divine Life Branches is not amassing wealth, name or fame. It is just to bring peace and harmony to the world by creating spiritual vibrations at various centres. Organise weekly meetings. Invite friends who are spiritually-inclined. Clear the doubts of the devotees. You can have a library with philosophical books. Invite learned men of your place to give discourses. Occasionally print my "Twenty Important Spiritual Instructions" and other leaflets for free distribution. Thus you can lay the seed for a Divine Mission. It will grow slowly and bring spiritual good to the world. This will contribute a lot to your own evolution and to the uplift of mankind as well."

(2) How to Start a Branch of The Divine Life Society

'Well begun is half-done.' I am not interested in gigantic plans and programmes. If there is a good beginning and if the workers have sincerity, faith and devotion, success is assured. I wrote to sincere students:—

"You have made a wonderful start and a good beginning It will strike root and bear blossoms soon. You can have the Yoga Class in a house, in a room. Make a signboard also. Hold meetings once a week. Collect some books from your friends and develop a library. I shall send you all my publications. To meet the ordinary expenses you can collect a small subscription from members. Have the following aims and objects:—

(a) To have Self-realisation through Yoga.

(b) To regenerate youths through Yoga Asanas, Pranayama and ethical training.

(c) To disseminate the Knowledge of Rishis and Yogins far and near.

(d) To develop universal brotherhood, cosmic divine love.

"Never be disheartened or diffident. There are many who have started a Branch of the Divine Life Society in their own homes. The members of the family join together in the morning and evening for common prayers and conduct Bhajans and Kirtans. The spiritual vibrations thus created bring peace and prosperity to the entire family. Do something among your own selected friends, even with two members."

I am ever ready to give detailed instructions to enthusiastic aspirants who are desirous of spreading the divine knowledge:—

"Collect a few members. Read some pages of my books. Clear the doubts of the aspirants. Make them do some Japa, Kirtan, meditation, study of the Gita. Ask them to maintain a spiritual diary and Likhita Japa notebook. You have got rare things and knowledge and capacities in which you have not sufficient confidence or of which you are not even aware. Express your hidden faculties. Give whatever you possess. The world will be benefited. Form a Group in your own place and start similar activities in different parts of the city. Do not waver. Be hopeful. You can do wonders. Radiate joy and peace. Have a definite line of work. Work a little. This will suffice. You can spend the time nicely, usefully. Let the flower blossom. The bees will come by themselves. Much effort is not needed. No effort is necessary. Simply press the switch; it will flow. I wish you success, freedom and perfection.

"Have meditation in the open air with select friends. Arrange group demonstration of Yoga Asanas. Have Trataka practice on OM or any of the Lord's pictures for 5 minutes. Introduce fasting or Phalahara on Ekadasi days. Give lessons on the various Chakras.

"Prepare the lessons daily at night, the previous day. Concentrate and collect ideas. Register and record them on a piece of paper or in a notebook. Read a paper if you cannot deliver a lecture. Speak slowly. Recharge yourself with mild Kumbhakas and Japa. Take good nutritious food and fruits.

"If you cannot give a fine speech, write an essay and read the paper with emphasis and great force from the bottom of your heart. Slowly you will gain the power of oration. When you meet good thirsty souls, give them good ideas and ask them to form such groups in their own places. That will facilitate your future work. Ask every man with whom you come in contact to read a few Slokas daily from the Gita and repeat the Gayatri Mantra. Initiate many. Eulogise the usefulness of Mantra and Japa. Introduce Malas for Japa."

(3) Spiritual Current Must Be Kept Alive

I carefully watch over the activities of the Branches and continue to inspire and encourage them every now and then. I send able and advanced aspirants to keep alive the current and spur them onward in their activities. Here are my instructions to one of them:

"How is the Centre now? Dead or gasping or full of life? Approach all Headmasters of High Schools and arrange for a magic-lantern Show of Yoga Asanas. Do not fail to do this work. I did this work in all schools of Punjab and the U.P. during my travels. Kindly send me a report of your activities now and then. Never make false excuses. Do not be diffident. Do not become a *Zanana* Vedantin. Through the work you do in schools and colleges spiritual Samskaras become imbedded in thousands of minds. That will burst forth when the time comes.

"Be bold. Even M.A's, Judges and Surgeons are worldly. You will be an Avatar before passionate people. Be bold and talk with nobility, humility and sincerity. You can electrify and spell-bind the audience. Assume a different strong personality on the platform. Throw fire, zeal and enthusiasm into your utterances. Do not lose any opportunity. Whatever you are doing now is sufficient to elevate the world. Do not wait to become a great Pundit to do this work.

"I am receiving several letters from the Branches you have visited and exhibited the Movie Films in Countless appreciations. No one has done such a work before. It is unprecedented. When the work taxes you, hide yourself in your own room or go to a solitary place for a change. Recharge the battery through silent meditation in seclusion and come out with redoubled energy. Regulate your energy. Do not pour all in at once. Take sufficient rest. Learn to relax. Hide yourself."

(4) Service Is Greater Than Meditation

"The present work you do is a greater Yoga than the important, so-called meditation (sleep and building air-castles combined) done by Vedantins of the present day. It is a great Yajna. Work like a lion. Roar like a lion. Congratulations on your noble work done in various Centres. It is all His Grace. Feel this. It is His Will that worked through your mind, intellect and body. Be grateful to Him always. Pray for His Blessings and Mercy. If anything is offered to you by devotees and admirers, do not refuse it under a false sense of Vairagya. Money is needed for work, medicine for the sick and publication work. Become a Maha Tyagi and Maha Bhogi. Take rest. Do not overwork. Regulate your energy. Drink, inhale much ozone. Do not mix with people. Talk a little on vital points only. As you are working hard, take great care of your health. Take plenty of milk, fruits, almonds. Take rest for a week. Rest means change of work and not sleeping and wasting time with useless friends or in aimless wanderings.

"Serve people whole-heartedly, willingly, untiringly, without grumbling, without showing even an occasional Sunday castor-oil face. This is rather difficult. Try your utmost. Then it will become pure Yoga. You need not meditate. You need not do Japa. You need not close the nostrils for Pranayama. Convert every motion, every breath, every movement of the body into pure Yoga as above described. It is service of the Lord. You work, live and breathe for Him alone. Entertain this Bhav. You will have cosmic consciousness soon. Remember this point: Work is worship. Work is meditation. Do not forget this. You will have to evolve through work and meditation. Scavenging is Yoga when done in the right spirit. The first duty before you is to place your head at the feet of all elders, Swamis and everyone in the Ashram, be he a scavenger or a Zamindar. Feel oneness. Be cheerful. Adjust. Bear injury and insults. Train the mind to be even in all circumstances and places. Then only can you be really strong."

(5) Integral Yoga

I do not encourage lop-sided development, but urge my disciples to combine the important branches of Yoga with emphasis on dynamic selfless service and cultivation of virtues, while yet giving the full scope of individual discretion to the aspirant:

"I do not press you to remain in cities. Your health and spiritual progress are very important. See how you have turned out solid work in such a short period. If you are still energetic and if you think that you can get on with the work with perfect ease, you can remain there for some more time. Or you can say 'Goodbye' to the city life. It is in your hands.

"You can come by the end of this month. Do not stay in cities longer. It will be detrimental to your interests and progress. You need seclusion now. Spend a long period in study also. Your present knowledge is shallow. Your inner nature also is not regenerated. Sadhana is needed. Now you need rest, a quiet life, in the Himalayan-Gangetic atmosphere for recharging the battery, for doing dynamic work with redoubled energy and vigour. Long stay in cities must be followed by a frequent change to secluded places. That will be beneficial to you. Kindly do come and stay here for a long period. Mere flying visits will not be of much benefit.

"Thou art blessed. God exists. God indwells everything. God is the Inner Ruler. God is to be realised. Dharma leads to God-vision. Goodness leads to God. Love leads to God. Meditate on the Eternal, thy, innermost Self or the Atman. Persevere in Sadhana. Plunge in Sadhana and meditation. Enter the silence. Become a flame of God. Attain eternal bliss through the Life Divine. He who lives for the service of others is very happy. He is blessed. He attains God-realisation. Service purifies the heart and brings the divine Light. Be rooted in the Atman. This is real Sadhana. Claim thy birthright amidst typewriting, editing books, writing articles. This is better than a cave-life. This is dynamic, integral Yoga. Though you are in the city, feel that you are in the Ashram here in the Himalayas. This is Yoga. This the test put by Janaka to Sri Suka."

(6) All-round Application to the Task

I want my disciples to be like myself in applying themselves in an all-round manner to the propagation of the message of the Lord and developing the divine qualities in themselves and inculcating them in others.

"Wherever you go, give, distribute, disseminate, your ideas, mottoes, ideals. Broadcast your spiritual feelings. Share with others. Always give, give, give. Give all. Ask nothing. Your usual routine for meditation and study must be kept up. Brahman alone is real. Minus Indriyas, you are Brahman "*Tat Tvam Asi*". I am not tired of repeating again and again these three ideas. They must enter your very nerves, cells, blood, bone. Hammer these ideas on the minds of all, along with Bhakti and Nishkama Karma. Carry these three ideas in your pocket, Chitta. This world, body, is shallow, Jalam, Svapna.

"Teach Asanas to thousands. Read my Brahmacharya article in all schools and colleges with demonstration of Asanas and Pranayamas. After silent meditation for 5 or 10 minutes, have Kirtan and OM chanting. Explain the Yogic and Vedantic terms to the members. The whole city will be charged with spiritual vibrations. Mere study of my writings with a little explanation of the Yogic terms will nicely constitute your Yoga Class. I have to remind you of:—

(a) Initiation into Mantra of as many thousands of students as possible.

(b) Introduction of Japa Mala.

(c) Kirtan and Bhajan at night.

(d) Study of the Gita, Atma-Bodha, Viveka-Chudamani, the Upanishads, etc.

(e) Printing some leaflets for free distribution.

"On Ekadasi day, arrange for a mass Hari Kirtan in a big Hall or Temple. Have a programme for short lectures by great men. Distribute Prasad at the end. Make necessary preparations seven days in advance. Thrill the world. This is an important and sacred work, wherever you go. This is a Divine Life Conference in small scale. You can do this, I know.

"You are doing wonderful work indeed. It is a beautiful beginning. This kind of combination of Japa, Kirtan, Yoga Asanas, study and lecture is the thing needed. Keep a memorandum book in your pocket. Note down all the points you have to attend to. By such work you can improve yourself. You will develop thinking. You will know Nature, Her ways. You will be more concentrated also when the mind is fully occupied. Thousands will be inspired to do some kind of religious performance. It is all purification of heart and Yoga for you.

"You can do real, silent, solid work through individual talks. It is a field for preparation and enlightenment for you. Work in various localities of the city must be taken up. It is not blind work. It is not business. It is His work done through your body and mind. In the course of five years you will excel many of the professors and renowned religious leaders, if you are sincere and do steady dynamic work."

CHAPTER SIX

SIVANANDA ASHRAM

Problems of Spiritual Organisations

Spiritual organisations with high aims and objects should be started only by Mahatmas who are absolutely free, perfect and unselfish. If religious institutions are started by selfish people, they become fighting centres and a menace to society and bring ruin to those who are associated with the workers. In the long run, through ill-managed institutions and Ashrams, people lose faith in God and religion and condemn all Mahatmas as pseudo Yogis. Sometimes selfish persons start spiritual institutions as business undertakings. They misguide the people.

Even an Ashram started by a self-realised person, with high aims and objects in the early stages may get polluted later on by mercenary motives. The founders must have extraordinary capacity to serve mankind. Then and then alone can real service be done at all times. When there is lack of interest and Sraddha in householders, it becomes difficult to carry on systematic work. Above all, it is extremely difficult to get workers with ability and devotion. These days aspirants do not appreciate much the value of selfless service. Many of the Ashrams suffer for lack of able workers.

The Ashram Grew by Itself

I never thought of starting an Ashram. When the great rush of students and devotees came to me for

(71)

spiritual guidance, with a view to render help to them and to make them useful to the world, I created some fields of activities for their evolution and for public good, encouraged them much in their studies and their Sadhana, and arranged necessary comforts and conveniences for their boarding and lodging, using the donations I received from some admirers for my personal use. Thus, in course of time, I found around me a huge Ashram and an Ideal Institution with congenial environment—a big Spiritual Colony—SHIVANANDA NAGAR.

I did not work with big plans or schemes. I did not approach any great person or Maharajah for getting money. The world appreciated the service done here on right lines. A little help came from the divine source and I carefully utilised every cent of it for bringing maximum spiritual good to the world. Several new palatial buildings crop up every year and yet there is lack of acommodation for the inmates and the stream of visitors. At every stage, there was splendid development of work. On many occasions devotees pressed me to undertake propaganda tours for collecting money. That was impossible for me. I take delight in giving and serving all. In 1940, grand arrangements were made for an extensive tour in the Punjab. I sent a telegram at once and cancelled the programrne. The telegraphic message conveys the attitude with which I manage the affairs of the Ashram:

"I do not care if the Divine Life Society flourishes or not. If it is the Grace of the Lord and if we carry on our Sadhana and service with the right attiude, Bhava and Sraddha, help is bound to come from Divine Source. Let me do as much as possible by remaining in my own small Kutir on the banks of the Ganga. When the honey is there, the bees will come by themselves. Shun ruthlessly the desire for money."

In a short period the work grew. Regular classes are now conducted on Yoga, Bhakti, Vedanta and Health. Today over 300 students live by my side with all comforts and conveniences, tread the path of Yoga, and serve the world in a variety of ways. Glory to the Lord. Blessed are the aspirants. Students of different cults and faiths come from various countries and stay with me for weeks and months. Devotees from all parts of India come to the Ashram frequently and join the collective Sadhana and Satsanga.

Where Everyone Is Welcome

As qualification for first class aspirants, Viveka, Vairagya, Shat-sampat and Mumukshutva are prescribed by the scriptures. Some orthodox cults have caste-restrictions and insist on the students passing through the four stages of life, viz., Brahmacharya, Grihastha, Vanaprastha and then Sannyasa. When students come to me, I do not enquire anything about their qualification, position, parentage, caste or capacity. I welcome even thieves and rogues, persons of tender age and those who are sickly and old also. I know very well that they will all become dynamic Yogis when they are put in the company of sages and saints or when they are allowed to stay in a place charged with marvellous spiritual vibrations.

Perfect Freedom

The spiritual vibrations of the Ashram have a great

benefical effect in moulding people in the path of Yoga. Thousands have felt this. I do not impose any rules or restrictions on the aspirants who desire to stay in the Ashram. Any number of persons can come and stay here as long as they like and they can go out the moment they wish. I do not demand any work, service or help from them. I permit them to carry on their own study and Sadhana and help them in all possible ways.

The highly devoted aspirants who appreciate selfless service for their own evolution spend all their time in carrying out useful works and manage the affairs of the Society nicely. It is all Yoga for them. They are all Yoga Bhrashtas, living examples and models for the world. Thousands of aspirants have come to the Ashram. Several hundreds have gone out, after proper training, either for intense Sadhana in seclusion or dynamic work in cities; and yet the Ashram is always full and every day at least a dozen highly educated candidates crave permission to live in the Ashram. The students are mysteriously helped by attending the Satsanga and taking bath in the holy Ganga. Through some work, they all come in close touch with me and learn a lot in a short period. Quickly they develop all divine qualities without much effort and become great Yogis.

Miracle of Miracles

How is it possible to run an ideal Ashram under the above circumstances? It is a great puzzle for many. It looks like a miracle to the world. People are staggered. I do not worry even a bit if the Secretaries and Managers of the Ashram come to me frequently with a big list showing a statement of debts extending to a lakh of Rupees. People's wonder knows no bounds when, in spite of such debts, I sanction the purchase of several automatic printing machines for the University Press, or latest model high class Cameras, Enlargers and Projectors for the Studio, or the construction of big halls, temples and Ghats by the side of the Ganga.

People complain that here they get more food and facilities than they need for their living. The inmates feel very rich and happy. Some may look as ordinary villagers; a few may not have had much education. But I find that every one who lives in the Ashram is a great saint with wonderful hidden faculties and talents. Prominent persons who visit the Ashram are stunned to see the wonderful development in the inmates, admire their capacities and enquire: "Dear Swamiji Maharaj, how do you find so many people of talents?"

Is there any instance of my having asked any inmate of the Ashram to go out or expressed ill-feelings or used harsh words to him? None at all. When I have serious complaints that a particular Sadhaka disturbs the peace of the Ashram or interferes with the smooth working of the institution, I ask the man to go out and live independently in some other suitable place. I give him enough money for travelling expenses and a note of introduction to devotees for helping him. I give him spiritual advice at the time of his departure and pray for his welfare and enlightenment. In a few days or weeks, the man feels the Ashram as his own sweet home and comes back with a changed angle of vision and heart. I heartily welcome him. I forget the past easily. I do not have a vindictive nature. I permit useless persons, pessimistic people and even those who criticise me and attack the management to stay in the Ashram. After a short stay, they are transformed miraculously. I see joy and bliss in their face.

How Aspirants Should Be Cared For

I have unlimited, spontaneous generosity, love and affection for all the students of Yoga, irrespective of their age or sex, qualifications or abilities. I am highly pleased with those who do Japa, or a little meditation or some kind of service for the society, the sick and the poor. I give ample scope for all types of people to remain in the Ashram and evolve through Sadhana or work for the spiritual uplift of mankind. I take special care of the old people, young aspirants and the helpless sick persons. I distribute sweets and fruits first to all of them and then take a small portion.

I remember now how I carried milk and curd to the old Sadhus in Swargashram and shampooed their legs and gave them medicine when they were sick. Even now I send a portion of my own food first to some Sannyasi students and visitors in the Ashram. For some years I myself carried a portion of my own food to a few hard workers who were taking a meager diet and had very poor health. Later on, when the work increased in all directions, I kept two young Brahmacharis by my side always to distribute fruits and biscuits to all the inmates of the Ashram. These were not thrown into the rooms in the way in which worldly people haughtily give charity. I had the Bhav that I served the Lord in that form. I did prostration first and then offered them.

When I occasionally send money or books or

eatables to my students at out-stations, I invariably say: "May this be kindly accepted." For spiritual attainment, the Bhav, the inner feeling and the motive are more important. This came to me naturally, and was not created consciously by any effort. It was not like the service done by egoistic people for name and fame. This one virtue of voluntarily serving the sick, the poor and the helpless with all humility is my main YOGA, and this one virtue alone helped me to develop all divine qualities and to see the Lord behind all names and forms.

Helpfulness and Love Towards All

Due to Prarabdha or Vikshepa of the mind, or a craving for sensual enjoyments or for some form of luxury, or a curiosity to see various places, people try to go away from the Ashram. Some advanced students after some years of stay in the Ashram, like to gain some experience from meditation in the interior parts of the Himalayas. I admire them and give them all facilities. They all depend on alms for their food, but I also send them enough money for their special milk and fruits. Some students who have a pushing nature desire to help humanity and desire to go out on lecture tours. I organise Spiritual Conferences and send such students to various centres.

In the Ashram, in the past, a few students with powerful senses and cravings, criticised me and abused the Ashram and the whole of the Himalayas and left the place in anger. I blessed them and prayed for light, knowledge and proper understanding and inner spiritual strength to them. But they all go out only to come back to the Ashram with a thorough change of heart. I welcome them with great love and affection. I forget the past quickly. Thus a man may go out a hundred times and come back. My love for the man is greater. It is not through compulsion or rules or regulations that men can be transformed into divine beings. They all must have convincing experiences of their own.

In the Ashram every one is in charge of some important section of work or other. When people go out suddenly, the work would naturally suffer. There would be a lot of irregularities when new persons handle the work. That might result a great loss also. I care only for the individual's progress and prosperity, knowledge and peace, and therefore do not stand in the way of any one who wishes to go out.

Individual Attention and Consideration

Some of the letters written by me to my students at out-stations several years ago explain how I care for my students:

I. Sri A. is wonderfully improving. He is the senior Acharya of the kitchen nowadays. He is the senior typist also. Kindly supply him with one set of the Upanishads, a fountain pen and a copy of my Practice of Vedanta from my account.

II. Kindly attend on Sri S.R.C. carefully. His health is already poor. He has some complaints now. His food is meagre. Kindly supply him saltish biscuits and fruits. He does not like sweets. May you ever abide in the Lord.

III. Whenever you are in need of money, write to me at once. In the name of Tapasya, do not spoil your health. You can do just as you like. Anyhow spend the time usefully. May Lord bless you.

IV. How is your health? Record all your experiences and send me a report of how you spend the 24 hours. My dear Yogiraj, you can return to the Ashram at any moment. This is your own spiritual home. For uninterrupted Sadhana and porfection, the following items are essential:

(a) Fine health through prayers, rest, relaxation with agreeable diet and Sadhana.

(b) A calm and cool place with spiritual vibrations.

(c) Simple food at regular intervals.

(d) Help of elderly persons and guidance from advanced students of Yoga or from Guru.

(e) Facility for medical aid in case of need.

These ensure quick spiritual progress. Without worry or anxiety, you can then progress nicely in the practice of Yoga. And you have all the above facilities here in the Ashram. May I send you money for your train fare? Cordial greetings.

Encouragement and Advice

I am always grateful to those who have served the Divine Mission. I value their services immensely and am ever lavish in showering praises. I also look to the personal necessities of my students—their health and spiritual evolution. Some years before, I wrote to one of my students:

I. Take great care of your health. You cannot live on grass, water and air alone. Give up this idea at once. Take nutritious food and plenty of energy-giving fruits. Learn to relax. This is very important. Go for a long, brisk walk. You have done solid work this year in the printing line. This will amply suffice. It is all His work. It is all His Grace. Feel this. Are you comfortable there? May I send you money for your personal expenses? Milk and nutritious food are needed when people work in the active field of dissemination of knowledge or do rigorous Sadhana in seclusion.

II. You have done miracles. It is not flattery. I never expected so much from you. Do not overwork. Regulate your energy. Take rest in suburbs when you are tired. On Ekadasi, hold Kirtans in different centres. Hold weekly classes. Have silent individual talks. You can influence people more by this method. Never sleep in householders' houses. RUN AWAY FROM LADIES. No play and joking with them.

III. Do not be afraid of the cold at Rishikesh. Do not be unneccssarily alarmed. You may use my blankets. Take milk and tea from the shop on my account. May you enjoy the Peace of the Eternal.

IV. Take rest. Do not work hard. Apply cooling oil on the head. Do Pranayama in the early morning when it is cool. It will recharge you with abundant energy. Take fruits also. Never neglect morning meditation and evening meditation. The goal of a Sannyasi is Vedantic Realisation, *Aham Brahma Asmi*. Brahma Nishtha is your food, drink and all in all. This can be kept up along with Karma Yoga.

I have great respect for the Sanskrit language and I encourage my students to study Sanskrit—whoever has an aptitude for it—though it may be at the cost of the Ashram itself. I wrote once to my student:

"If I posses a ghost or a tree that bears currency notes and coins as fruits, I can easily satisfy these Sanskrit students. Their needs are endless. I have to do something for helping them. They are doing wonderful research work and have deep study. Their study will seriously be interferred with if the books are not provided. I wish to start a Sanskrit College with a large number of students and arrange all facilities for the Sannyasi students to do research work in Sanskrit literature. We should have mercy and must serve others at the sacrifice of our wants even. It is my inborn nature. That is the Dharma of a saint."

Spirit of Accommodation

When one of my students had left the Ashram for some reason, I at once felt that his valuable experience and faculty should not be lost for the service of humanity. So I wrote thus:—

"I was sending you money for your pocket expenses. The money was returned with the remark: 'Left the Place.' I am always at thy feet to serve you at all times. You only refuse it. Why should you depend on anybody, when I am here to serve you in all ways? Why should you live in cities with worldly persons? There are various sections here in which you can work, gently, mildly, slowly, a little, without mixing with anybody, independently, having connections with me only.

"All sections of work suffer for want of people and proper supervision. Even if you look after a little work in the correspondence section, it will be a great help to the world. You can assist me in a hundred ways. Do not work hard as before. You do a little work without any responsibility. This is God's Blessing and Grace. Take plenty of rest and do a little work. You can remain away from the Ashram. Your food will be placed in your room. I shall give you money for your expenses.

"There is no dearth for food for you here. I do not refuse food to any one. Why should you live in cities? Gradually you will lose all your faculties when you are not in touch with work. The worldly atmosphere is not congenial to spiritual progress. Therefore come at once to Rishikesh. May I send you train fare? If you like, you can live here for six months and six months in cities.

"If you change your outlook, vision, imagination and attitude a bit, you can be happy here and everywhere. Man suffers on account of his own imagination and his old habit of thinking. He never allows himself to be changed. This is Maya. Adjust and adapt. Be happy and cheerful at all times. Evolve quickly and become a dynamic Yogi and bring Light and Knowledge to the whole world."

Who Can Start Ashrams

An Ashram is a Glorious centre to ensure World Peace. Many enthusiastic persons start Ashrams with a fine letterhead. That is not enough. The starting of new Ashrams by beginners will not bring good results to the world. It needs special faculties to run an Ashram successfully. For beginners, that will be a hindrance, and for advanced students that will be a downfall. Many years ago, some Sannyasins wrote to me for financial help and advice for improving the activities of their Ashrams, and the reply I gave to one of them is reproduced below. That clearly explains my attitude and principles:

"Beloved Swamiji, your achievements, ambitions, aims and objects are laudable, indeed. O Swamiji, aspire not for Gurudom, comforts, name and fame when you start an Ashram or a religious Society. Generally those who start Ashrams are humble in the beginning and do some service. When they become rich and well established, they care not for public service or individual evolution. They become arrogant and autocratic. Beware of temptations and work as a meek Sevak always. Even after Self-realisation, leave not the daily routine of Sadhana.

"I do not know any rich Rajah or Zamindar. I have no disciples. Some aspirants who want real spiritual training, consider me as their Guru. I take great care of them. That is all. I cannot help you with money. I am serving the world by a variety of ways and work through all Ashrams, Mutts and religious institutions.

"If you do public service with a selfless spirit, if people see the spirit of renunciation in you, then they themselves will volunteer to help you in every way. Do not move heaven or earth for money. Try not your luck through Derby Sweep. It is a pity for Sadhus to think of such schemes.

"Nowadays aspirants do not care to look to their spiritual progress. They shave their head, colour their clothes and remain at Rishikesh for some time and then pass for great Yogis. They begin to collect money for starting Ashrams for leading a comfortable life.

"There are enough Ashrams and Mutts in India. Sincere, selfless workers are rare. Before one starts an Ashram, one must have been leading an exemplary life. His very presence must give peace, power and bliss to all. Only then can one successfully run the institution.

Ideals Must Not Be Forgotten

"Before starting an Ashram, the mottoes, ambitions and aims are no doubt grand, charming and attractive. As soon as a little fund and fame come, the ideal is forgotten. The spirit of selfless service dwindles away. The objects are abandoned. The Founders want to lead a comfortable life with some chosen disciples and followers. Even granting that the founders are able to live an ideal life, their disciples will not be able to manage it with the same spirit later. It becomes a place of quarrel or a business-house. The head of the Ashram and the inmates there should lead a life of Vairagya, absolute renunciation. The Ashram run by such people stands as a centre, a nucleus of perennial peace, bliss and joy. It attracts everyone. Millions all over the world derive inspiration. The world is always in need of such Ashrams.

"Every Sannyasi, every Yogic student has got some defect or other. It is only a full-blown Yogi who will be absolutely free from evil qualities and defects. All are in the path of evolution. Everybody is likely to err sometimes, even very often. Become tolerant. See good in everything. Slight rupture or friction is bound to come between friends and workers, at times between Sannyasins, too. One must excuse the other, must reunite and forget the past. You must have a tendency to grasp only the good in others and try to emphasise it in your everyday life. No one is entirely bad. Remember this point well. You must have

adaptability when you mix with others. Have perfect
control over impulses. Only then will more workers
feel happy to live with you and serve your Ashram.
May the noble Mission established by you gloriously
prosper. I shall be always happy to help you."

CHAPTER SEVEN

LIGHT ON THE PATH OF RENUNCIATION

The Glory of Renunciation

Every Religion has a band of anchorites who lead the life of seclusion and meditation. There are Bhikkus in Buddhism, Fakirs in Mohammedanism, Sufistic Fakirs in Sufism, Fathers and Reverends in Christianity. The glory of a religion will be lost if there are no monks leading a life of renunciation and service to the world. It is these people that maintain the religions of the world. They give solace to the householders when they are in trouble and distress. They are the harbingers of peace and wisdom. They heal the sick, comfort the forlorn and bring help to the hopeless, joy to the depressed, strength to the weak, and knowledge to the ignorant. One true Sannyasin can change the thought-currents of the world for better.

A real Sannyasi is a mighty potentate of this earth. Sannyasins have done sublime work in the past. They are working wonders at present. One real Sannyasin can change the destiny of the whole world. I dance in joy when I see or hear from an aspirant who entertains genuine devotion, aspiration and inclination for the path of renunciation and tries to get out of this quagmire of Samsara. Through prayers and thought-currents I am in very close touch with such students and help them a lot. They are all attracted towards me and leave the world quickly with a great

(86)

hope for the future. I welcome them with great joy and train them nicely in a variety of ways in the path of Yoga and take care of them until they are able to stand firm in the path.

Youth Is the Best Period for Renunciation

In scriptures, the order of Sannyasa is mentioned for those who have passed the Brahmacharya, Grihastha and Vanaprastha stages of life. That means, people took Sannyasa in their old age, on the verge of death. It is quite good to have some peace at the time of death. By this they may get a good birth. From experience I find that tremendous energy is needed for purposes of contemplation, clear vision and extraordinary purity of body, mind and heart. I consider youth, with abundant energy and mental purity, as the foremost qualification for the path of renunciation. I have all admiration for those young Brahmacharis who do not have any worldly bondage and entanglements. They can be moulded nicely.

Viveka, Vairagya, Shat-sampat and Mumukshutva are the primary qualifications to students prescribed by the scriptures. It will not be possible to have all the above qualifications when people live in worldly environments with heavy responsibilities, anxieties and worries. By the time they develop one virtue or try to remove a single defect or evil in the mind, they get entangled in various other directions. The vibrations of the materialistic world are not favourable for spiritual progress in the early stages. They have to spend their entire energy solely in resisting the temptations. Therefore I prefer young persons. Necessary qualifications will come by themselves when they tread the path of Yoga, in a favourable atmosphere, and when they live in the company of Yogis, in a place far away from the temptations and attraction of sense-objects.

No Rigid Conditions Are Attached

I heartily welcome all types of people. Old people can take bath in the holy Ganga and spend their time in · prayers and Bhajan and enjoy the benefits of Satsanga. Young persons will evolve quickly through a dynamic Sadhana and bring spiritual good to the world. If people only show some symptom of disgust for sensual enjoyment coupled with a taste for the path of Yoga, I at once give them Sannyasa and share with them what I have and encourage them to a great extent.

It is a great surprise to many. to see that I give initiation through post also. Some students who are not in a position to come to the Himalayas have taken Sannyasa by receiving the sacred cloth and instructions by post. I cannot express their joy in full. They have made wonderful progress. I closely watch them.

The entire voluntary donation I receive from devotees for my personal use is spent in providing comforts and conveniences to the students, for their welfare and peace and in creating hundreds of avenues in which they can quickly evolve and help the world in a variety of ways. In my method of work for the spiritual uplift of mankind, I permit even married people to take to the path of renunciation and live like Sannyasins. There are many who have taken to the order of Sannyasa when they have a family and children. After some training here, they go back and live near the family or a little away and take care of the family with complete detachment and gloriously prosper in their Sadhana.

The point of my method is that I look to the motive and the inner purity of the seeker. I do not impose too many rules and restrictions on food and dress. External conformity to rules is not of much value. My students can live in any place, in any dress and yet effectively follow my instructions. They all set an example to the whole world. Glory to the true, ideal Sannyasin who leads an exemplary life. This world is in need of ideal Sannyasins who will serve the country and humanity with divine consciousness and disseminate true knowledge and carry the message of the Sages and Saints to every door. May Sannyasins, the repositories of divine knowledge, the torch-bearers of Truth, the beacon-lights of the world, the corner-stones of spiritual edifices and the central pillars of the eternal Dharma or religion, guide the nations of the world.

Who Are Fit to Be My Disciples

Though I give much freedom and liberty in dress and external forms, I am very strict with my students with regard to the essentials. The rules prescribed by the Order of Sannyasa must be followed. Then only can they shine as ideal Sannyasins. Comfortable Sannyasa is very dangerous. They should not give lenience to the mind. Fashionable, independent Sannyasins are a menace to society. The people in the world curse such Sannyasins and treat them with disrespect and contempt. They, however exalted in the spiritual line, should not live in the company of women or householders and freely mix with others.

Burning Vairagya with simple living and high thinking must be the ideal at every moment of their lives.

No doubt renunciation is mental. That does not mean that you can do anything and live in any way you like. That will bring your downfall. Strive for perfection by following the traditional rules for discipline and control of mind and senses. Discipline in food and dress will naturally manifest itself if you have genuine Vairagya and dispassion. External observance of the rules will help you to stick to the path. Maya works havoc. Maya deludes. Beware. Be cautious at every step and watch the Vrittis of the mind.

My disciples should have no superiority complex. They are not dry philosophers who spend all their time and energy in preaching alone. They have self-sacrifice and serve the world with their silent and intense Sadhana. In the midst of intense service, they learn the way to rivet the mind on the Lakshya. They are rooted in the idea: "The world is a long dream (Deergha Svapna), perishable—Truth alone is Real." For my students, there is no world. They perceive the Divinity behind all names and forms.

Purify the Inner Nature

Purify your mind. Develop Sattvic qualities such as nobility, courage, magnanimity, generosity, love, straightforwardness, truthfulness. Eradicate all evil qualities such as lust, greed, anger, avarice, Raga-dvesha and other negative traits which stand in your way of ethical perfection and Self-realisation. Ethical perfection is a pre-requisite to Self-realisation. No amount of practice can be of any value to the aspirant if he ignores this side of Sadhana. Love all. Prostrate yourself before everybody. Become humble. Talk loving, sweet, endearing words. Give up selfishness, pride, egoism, hypocrisy. Regenerate your lower nature.

Find out through self-introspection if you want real freedom and liberation or you are just inquisitive about higher things or have a lurking desire for obtaining money, name and fame by exhibiting spiritual powers. Become sincere. All qualifications will come by themselves when you are in the company of evolved persons and live in an atmosphere charged with spiritual vibrations.

Attitude Towards Women

My silent adorations and prostrations to all women, who are manifestations of the Divine Mother, Sakti or Kaali. They are the backbone of society and upholders of religion. If they are inspired, the whole world will be inspired. There is a peculiar religious instinct in them. They have natural, inborn divine qualities. In olden days, Hindu ladies also led the life of celibacy, served the Rishis, meditated on the Atman and obtained Brahma Jnana. In ancient days there were many Siddhas, Brahma Jnanis, Vairagis, Bhaktas and advanced Yogis among women. By their purity and perfection they could do miraculous things when there were occasions for utilising their spiritual power. There are instances of their giving life to the dead, stopping the rising of the sun in the morning and of controlling the elements also. Even today you can find many women in Rishikesh, Haridwar, Brindavan, Banaras and other holy places in India, who have renounced the world and taken to the path of Yoga.

I do not detest anybody. I revere a woman as my own self. I regard women as Mother Durga or Divine Mother. Women are dynamic forces on earth. Religion is sustained through their piety. To passionate youths, I have written a lot about the perishable nature of the physical body of women. It is just to develop in them a strong Vairagya and help control of their senses and mind. Though for the sake of inducing Vairagya in men I have given a negative description of women, I have great reverence for them. I serve them. I have done Kirtans with them in various Sankirtan Sammelans in the Punjab and the U.P. Many ladies come to the Ashram from Delhi and other places even if they get two or three days' holidays. They come in groups and join the daily Satsanga and enjoy the peace and bliss, and stay within the Ashram for days and weeks.

Should Women Renounce the World

No doubt it is difficult for young women to get on in the Sannyasa line. They do not have the same liberty and freedom as men. Men can live and move about in any way and sleep anywhere. They can go from door to door for alms and maintain themselves. But women are greatly at a disadvantage and suffer thereby. It is a pity that there are not many ideal institutions in India exclusively for women where they can live peacefully, serve the world and evolve. Ideal institutions with all comforts and conveniences for women, who are spiritually-inclined, are a great need of the hour. For ages, this important work has been neglected.

I get letters from some sincere cultured ladies expressing a desire to tread the path of renunciation. In 1936, I gave a reply to a devotee giving my helpful suggestions:

"I cannot safely suggest any Ashram where you can live peacefully and evolve. You should get a decent amount from your parents. Invest it in a Bank. You can lead a simple life with the interest you get from the deposit. This is the best way. Even then, live in an Ashram where you have advanced souls, Mahatmas, or live with some elderly ladies of a religious temperament. Devote all your time to the study of the Upanishads, the Gita and to Sadhana. Specialise in Kirtan and Bhajan. When you advance on the spiritual path, you can go from village to village and elevate the masses and develop Bhakti in them. The world will worship you if you do so. If this is not possible, you can get a monthly allowance from your brother. This will make you dependent on him and you will develop a leaning mentality. You must be expecting his sympathy every month. This is not safe.

"If you are bent upon treading the path of renunciation but cannot manage independent means for your maintenance, you can give private tuition to some girls. Their parents will support you in return. I do not mean that you should become a qualified mistress of a school or a nurse. That is worldly. That will take away all your time and you cannot have strength or energy to do intense, regular Sadhana. The temptations of the world will affect you in the long run. Vairagya will slowly vanish. Luxury and comforts will creep in. You will miss the Goal. You will not be able to keep up the same mind and Bhav as now if you lead a comfortable life and freely mix with worldly persons. Be adamant. Never change your mind. Have perfect trust in God."

Service to Women

"This mission of service to sincere women is very dear to my heart. I do not have money. I have no knack to collect money from the public, from Rajahs and Zamindars and businessmen. I do not go out for collecting money in the name of service. Occasionally I receive a little money from devotees. I spend this voluntary donation for the spiritual uplift of those who are around me and those who keep themselves in close touch with me from various centres. My books are sold in large numbers in many parts of the world, but I do not earn anything from the publications. I lavishly give away my books free. I do not know business. For starting an institution purely for ladies, I do not have resources or facilities at present."

Some orthodox people and Sannyasis say that women are not fit for the path of renunciation. My view is different. They too are eligible to tread the path of Yoga and renunciation. Several times I have thought of concentrating more on rendering a real service to mankind by starting an Ashram exclusively for ladies. That will be a boon to the world. In the absence of proper support from the world for an ideal institution exclusively for women, I have permitted many educated and cultured ladies to live in this Ashram. I personally attend to their needs and train them in all branches of Yoga, Bhajans and Kirtans.

Many have learnt Yoga exercises and derived incalculable benefits.

Among them, there are many from foreign countries also. I give them initiation into the Order of Sannyasa. After some training in the Ashram they go back to various centres and they continue their Sadhana and service to the world. The Divine Life Society Branches have Ladies' sections in all parts of the world, where they have ample scope not only for their own evolution but also for serving womankind. The ladies who stay in the Ashram have all comforts and conveniences. They have all facilities, liberty and freedom. In the absence of a separate Ashram exclusively for women, this Institution has become an ideal centre for their spiritual evolution. May they all prosper and enjoy peace and Divine Glory and Splendour.

To Those Who Wish to Take Sannyasa

Many sincere seekers of Truth in different parts of the world write to me very often expressing their eagerness to take to the path of renunciation or the Order of Sannyasa. From experience I have found that many of those who renounce the world on account of the emotional type of Vairagya, which might have been induced special reason or other, eventually fail to keep up to the spirit of renunciation and consequently go back to the world or become a disgrace to the Order of Sannyasa. While to those who have genuine Vairagya and burning aspiration, I recommend immediate renunciation; others I advise as follows, in order to give them ample opportunity to develop their Vairagya and prepare themselves for the path:—

Worldly greatness is nothing. It is a child's play. You must become a great man in the spiritual field. Remain in the world, but be not worldly-minded. Mere college study cannot make you great. When you remain in the world, prepare yourself nicely for the path of Sannyasa. You have Vairagya, but you have no experience in the line. I am ready to give you Sannyasa at any moment. Suppose you remain with me as a Sannyasi, have you got the strength to face your mother, wife, sister and brothers when they weep bitterly with a broken heart in front of my Kutir? Think well and decide this point. Destroy Moha first. Occasionally go out and live in a secluded place for a month or two, away from your family and see if your mind often goes to your people, your property and native place. Test your mental strength.

Mere emotion and enthusiasm will not serve you much in the path of renunciation. The path of Sannyasa is beset with many difficulties. But it is full of joy and bliss and is smooth for the man of firm determination, patience and fortitude. The life of a Sannyasi is the best kind of life in the world. A true Sannyasi is the real monarch of the three worlds. Even a mere aspirant is an Emperor of the three worlds. Have courage. Be bold. Realise that the world is a mere illusion. Assert your real Satchidananda Svarupa.

Sit for a moment alone in a quiet room. Enquire. Cogitate and investigate. Realise the glory of living in the Atman. Introspect. Try to remove your defects and weaknesses. This is real Sadhana.

In the early stages of your life, do intense Sadhana in seclusion and a little service to

Mahatmas, the sick and the poor—as much as you can. Do not think of conducting classes on Yoga and preaching and presiding over big Conferences. Do not entertain the idea of a world tour and of becoming a World-Teacher. All such hopes will only result in a downfall. When you are young, do intense Sadhana and have deep study. Forget the past and the future. Lord Jesus hid himself in solitude for several years. He came out for a period of three years to electrify and thrill the world with his spiritual powers and illumination. Empty bullets in the air cannot influence the birds. The words of a man who has no ethical and spiritual development will be like empty bullets. They cannot have any influence on worldly minds. Become a dynamic personality. Through pure thought (Satsankalpa) you can revolutionise the materialistic world. Do not be tempted by name and fame or comforts and conveniences. Lead a hard life.

Combine Service and Meditation

There is one difficulty when you live in a jungle or a cave. As you are a neophyte, you do not know how to regulate your energy and adjust your daily routine and spend the time profitably. You do not know how to get over depression when it manifests itself. Beginners cannot spend all the twenty-four hours in meditation alone. They have to work in the beginning for purification of the heart as well. They should combine work and meditation. I have never come across people in all my experiences of this life who always remained in meditation entirely and who emerged from it with flying colours. What I want to emphasise is that beginners cannot fare well in seclusion. They become Tamasic and lose their talents and hidden faculties after a long stay in seclusion.

Financial Independence

I have closely studied the lives of Sannyasins, and I have come to the definite conclusion that a little money helps the Sadhaka in his Sadhana and evolution. Financial independence will bring peace of mind and strength during the Sadhana period. Downfall comes only when you try to augment the amount and to accumulate a bank balance. Yet, if you have a strong power of endurance, patience and fine health, if your Vairagya is intense and of a sustained type and if you are willing to do some selfless service to mankind, you need not worry about money. You can renounce the world even this moment. It is not advisable to waste your precious life in trying to earn more and saving a lot. There is plenty everywhere for sincere Sadhakas. Leave the world quickly. Fly, fly away from the company of worldly-minded persons. Get away from the bustle of cities and the tumultuous world. Run quickly to solitary places like Rishikesh. You will be outside the danger zone.

Good Sadhus are well looked after everywhere. It is only the beggars who come in the garb of Mahatmas that become a nuisance to the public. It is not easy for the public to differentiate Mahatmas from beggars by a mere casual look. But it is quite possible to find out real Mahatmas from their talk, walk and action. These days Sraddha is lacking among householders. To avoid interruptions in Sadhana I ask the students to keep enough money with them to meet their needs. Do not entertain the begging mentality. If possible provide for bare necessities or join some Ashram or religious institutions.

Importance of Service

As a drastic measure to overcome the vicious nature and worldly Samskaras, I ask the students to drown themselves in active service for some months or years. This enables them to forget the past entirely and devote their entire energy and time to spiritual pursuits. They forget their body and surroundings. They train their mind to behold automatically the hidden essence behind all names and forms. They learn to keep a balanced state of mind under all conditions of life, pleasant or painful. The period of training varies according to the evolution and standard of the students.

In my method, every student should learn cooking, washing, nursing, serving the Sadhus, Mahatmas and the sick in all possible ways. They must spend hours in deep study, meditation, Japa and prayers. Even during work they should do mental Japa. They should learn to adjust and adapt themselves to various circumstances and persons. They all must learn typewriting and first-aid also. They should learn Bhajans and Kirtans and must prepare fine essays and articles on Yoga and Vedanta. I prescribe all the important items of Sadhana for a quick spiritual evolution and give them all facilities and comforts. When I find some progress in them, I send them to some cool places for deep meditation.

Sannyasins and Politics

In these days of political agitation, even Sannyasins are asked by political leaders to join the agitation. It is a sad mistake. These leaders have not understood the glory and significance of the life of pure Nivritti Marga. These Sannyasins purify the world, even though they remain in the caves of the Himalayas, by their thought-vibrations. They help the world better. My field is the spiritual path. Let the politicians and scientists work in their own fields. It may be that you cannot separate politics from religion. But different people should work in different fields according to their capacity and temperament. All are important and great in their own fields.

Is Guru Indispensable

Only genuine, thirsty spiritual aspirants know me.

Aspirants need not be afraid of pitfalls and snares in the spiritual path. The whole spiritual world is ready to back up sincere students who are trying to lift up their head from the quagmire of Samsara. Aspirants should nourish their good Samskaras through Japa and regular meditation.

Even in this materialistic age, India is full of thirsty aspirants who want God and God alone, who are ready to give up wealth, family and children, ruthlessly, for the sake of God-realisation which they regard as the be-all and end-all of their existence. This is a land of sages and saints. Thousands of seekers after Truth are in close touch with me from all parts of the world. Many foreigners come to India in search of Yogis and Mahatmas. Glory to India and all devotees.

The spiritual path is beset with many obstacles. The Guru who has already trodden the path will guide the aspirants safely and remove all sorts of obstacles and difficulties. A personal Guru is therefore necessary.

There is no more powerful way of overcoming the vicious nature and old Samskaras in the aspirants than personal contact with and service to the Guru. Guru's Grace will, in a mysterious manner, enable the disciples to perceive the spiritual power within, though it is impossible for the Guru to point out God or Brahman to be this or that.

Initiation Transforms the Mind

Initiation (Diksha) is not a mere change in outward forms. Real change of mind and clear vision and understanding come to the aspirant after the initiation by a Brahmavidya Guru. Many students, according to their own fancy, select their own method of Sadhana without considering the consequences. Improper diet, wrong Sadhana without a proper guide, hard and foolish austerities on a weak body, torturing the body in the name of Tapasya, have entirely ruined many aspirants. Therefore a personal Guru is necessary to give timely instructions according to the change of seasons, circumstances and progress.

The grace of a Guru is necessary. That does not mean that the disciple should sit idle. A Guru can clear the doubts, show the spiritual path best fitted to the aspirants and inspire them. The rest of the work will have to be done by the aspirants themselves. It is foolish to think that one can have all Siddhis (psychic powers) and Mukti from a drop of water from the Kamandalu of a Mahatma or a Yogi. There is no magic pill for attaining Samadhi. It is mere delusion to think so.

First Deserve, Then Desire

To find out a Guru who may sincerely look after the interests of his pupil is a difficult task in this world. It is quite true. But to find out a disciple who will act sincerely according to the instructions of his Guru is also a very, very difficult task.

As disciples are arrogant, disobedient and self-willed in these days, no senior man in the spiritual path wishes to accept disciples for training. They bring only troubles to the Guru. They do not want to carry out the instructions of the Guru. They become Gurus themselves in a few days. This problem of Guru and disciples is indeed an embarrassing one. If you cannot find a first class type of Guru, at least try to find out one who has been treading the path for some years, who is compassionate and selfless and who will take a special interest in your welfare and progress.

Realised souls are not rare. Ignorant, worldly-minded persons cannot easily recognise them. Only a few persons who are pure and have all virtues can understand realised souls. They alone will be benefited in their company.

There is no use of running hither and thither in search of realised men. Even if the Lord Krishna remains with you, He cannot do anything for you, unless you are fit to receive Him.

To serve God and mammon at the same time is impossible. You will have to sacrifice the one or the other. You cannot have light and darkness at the same time. If you want to enjoy spiritual bliss, you will have to renounce sensual pleasures.

Even if one of my disciples lifts up his head from the quagmire of Samsara, I have justified my existence. The greatest service that I can do to humanity is training and moulding aspirants. Every Yogic student, when he is purified and elevated, becomes a centre of spirituality. He will draw to himself, through his magnetic aura, thousands of baby souls for spiritual transformation and regeneration.

Students who are in the world with responsibilities, need not wait for obtaining a Guru. They should select their own Ishta Devata and a Mantra suitable to their taste and do Sadhana and prayers. At the proper time, a Guru will appear to them. It is better to receive the Mantra from a Guru. The Mantra received from the Guru has a mysterious influence.

CHAPTER EIGHT

JNANA YAJNA

Profound Experiences Blossom
As Countless Publications

When I study scriptures, I mark the important portions. I constantly think over the points and reflect. I found effective methods to tide over difficulties and obstacles. I recorded my own experiences. Thousands came to me in person or through correspondence seeking a remedy for solving their problems. I gave suggestions and suitable remedies based on my own experiences. I do not miss a single thought because I record all my thoughts. I attach great value to the experiences of the students also. I minutely observe and note down the points for the benefit of other students. I take care to see that these reach immediately all aspirants at distant places through my letters, articles and messages, through all leading journals and periodicals in various languages.

For the guidance of so many struggling souls, I released my experiences as 'Mind, Its Mysteries and Control', 'Spiritual Lessons', 'Precepts for Practice'. I classify the lessons and publish the same in pamphlet and book form. Thus my publications become numerous and limitless. When once I gave a lot of new material for 'Practice of Yoga', Volume Second, the publishers gave me a suggestion to have only one volume. In 1933, I wrote to them:

"Why do you stop my work? Let 'Practice of Yoga'

(104)

be in several Volumes, 3, 4, 5 and so on, when I have brand new ideas and lessons. Let me work as long as my eyes are good, as long as I have new messages and lessons for seekers after Truth. My love to serve mankind is so great that I will continue the publication work with the help of able stenographers and secretaries even if I lose my eyesight. Let the Divine work grow and bring peace and bliss to the world "

Why There Are Repetitions in My Books

I believe in the harmonious development of heart, intellect, mind and body. One-sided development is not of much benefit. I do not ignore any of the teachings of the sages and saints of various religions and cults. For a quick spiritual progress of students of different tastes and temperaments, I give the essence from all sources. I call this "Synthesised Yoga" or "Integral Yoga." The lessons that I give are the outcome of my own researches and also the experiences of thousands of devotees.

In all my books I emphasise the essential points of the practical side for an all-round development. This is regarded by some as "Repetition." They are very helpful to sincere students. Aspirants are able to grasp the value and importance of such useful repetitions. These lessons are intended to create a deep and indelible impression on the minds of the aspirants. While describing a particular subject, with a view to making the book useful to all the readers, I repeat the vital points that are to be observed in daily life. These prove to be very helpful. They hammer the mind that is tossed by materialistic influences. That helps to develop the will-power also. There is a message for the solace, peace, freedom and perfection of every individual.

Devotees have a big library with a complete set of my books and yet they frequently write to me for books that are in the press. They very often write to me: "The one beauty I find in your books is that the lessons create a taste for spiritual progress and tempt me to follow some of the lessons, though I am conscious that I do not have a natural taste or inclination for the path. The lessons are meant for me and I find them highly useful for my material progress as well. I feel a new power and hope in me after reading a few pages of your book: 'Mind, Its Mysteries and Control'."

In 1935 the publishers sent me a letter from a devotee who complained that my books contain a lot of repetitions. I wrote to them: "Repetition should be carefully avoided. You will have to sit 3 or 4 nights with full thermos flasks of tea and work hard for removing the repetitions. For fear of repetition, do not omit the important portions. Repetitions are necessary when the lessons aim at hammering the worldly mind. This world is a sphere of repetition. We cannot please the entire world. The Gita, the Upanishads and other scriptures are full of repetitions. This cannot be avoided. Without hammering, nature refuses to change. After some years, when we bring out fresh editions, we can thoroughly overhaul each and every book, every para, every sentence and improve the book. **Print all that I have given you. Do not omit even a single comma or word.**" The devotee of that letter says that my books are full of repetitions and yet he wants to have a complete list of my latest publications! At the end he adds: 'It is food and life for me.'

It will be a great surprise for the world to see that I authorise any number of publishers to bring out new editions of several of my books. One and the same book comes out from various presses in India, Germany, Switzerland, Indonesia and America. I want the maximum amount of work in a short space of time. My letters written in 1934-36 explain the method of my work in carrying out a dynamic work through the press:—

"I like 20 days' and 10 days' productions. Can you do 'Dhana-dhan' or 'Fata-fut' work? Can you take up 3 or 4 books at a time? Engage several presses. This is Dhana-dhan work which is being done by a small press here in Rishikesh. Mind not about payments. Anyhow the bills will be paid, sooner or later."

"Engage several presses for finishing the matter quickly. Do not rely on one Press alone. Press people, goldsmiths and tailors belong to the same category. They do things very slowly, leisurely. They do not stick to their promise."

My object is quick work and rapid dissemination of spiritual knowledge. This is indicated in my next letter.

Rapid Work Is My Ideal

I am not restrictive about my publications. Any good matter must be shared with the readers at once for their prompt spiritual benefit. I do not want my readers to wait until a new publication is ready. Hence, if any new ideas crop up, I at once add them in the latest work under print even though they may not have a direct connection with the subject-matter of the book. Nor do I wish that valuable time should be wasted in carefully scrutinising every word.

"Do not worry about the mistakes in printing. You need not be afraid of mistakes. If you send me the proof, I shall correct them. Do not confine the book to 125 pages. If you have good matter, insert it and increase the price of the book by a few annas. What harm is there if there are 200 or 300 pages in a book? You can help the world by bringing out substantial and authoritative works."

Where a recognition of merit is due, I am not hesitant about expressing it:

"The book 'Yoga Asanas' is beautiful. It has got its own charm in the field, though there are many books in the market."

Attention to Details

I am also very careful in giving detailed instructions:

"You can introduce meditation on OM (figure) itself. This is both Saguna and Nirguna meditation. Print some nice OM Charts and as footnote write some instructions on concentration and meditation. Insert the Four Mahavakyas also on four sides. I wish to have a Japa leaflet: Print OM 108 times on a page. Those who do not like to have a Japa Mala can go through this page."

❂   ❂   ❂

"Herewith a detailed article on Brahmarandhra. This will suffice. The elaborate description of Pericarp, Nibodhaka fire, Nirvana Sakti, etc. does not help the student much. It is all Greek and Latin—Mystic. Do not take any matter from any other books. Whatever I have written is quite sufficient. Do not copy matter from any other source and spoil the beauty of the books."

  ✿   ✿   ✿

I carefully watch over the way my books are brought out. Sometimes, the publishers thought of omitting some of the portions they did not consider to be apposite or appropriate. But I do not wish any valuable matter to be lost in this process. Hence, in the following letter I emphasised their importance and also asked them to be careful about preserving the force of the writing which might be lost in the process of changing the language I do not like too much of correction and editing.

"You can remove some portions. But remember, it is not the language or style but the power behind the thought that influences people. In trying to improve the language, etc., the force must be kept up. Whenever you make a change, you must reflect over the views of the writer. Mere metaphysical or flowery decoration will not make any improvement. The force of the writer must never be lost. Keep this in view when you think of any improvement in the publications."

The following observations would show how I appreciate a good production and also how I am disinclined to deletions:

"The book is very beautiful with the Introduction. You may think that you get some 'criticism' from the press. This is only a wrong imagination. Some newspapers will praise the volume. If you insert a thrilling advertisement, the copies will be sold like hotcakes. Coupled with 'Practice of Vedanta', this will form a fine combination for the study of Vedanta."

    ❀   ❀   ❀

"In 'Yoga Asanas', there is a great difference between the 1st and the 2nd editions. You have omitted all Sanskrit words like 'Parichchinna Ananda, Bimba Ananda', etc. Sanskrit words have great, special power and significance. On account of the contagion from the editor of a humorous Weekly, you have omitted the Sanskrit words. In future, kindly do not omit even a single syllable. There is a force, beauty and elegance in Sanskrit words. It will not in the least break the continuity of thought while reading."

No Attachment to Copyright

I do not expect any royalty from publishers. For dynamic work, I ask all the publishers to bring out several editions of my books in different languages. I do not demand anything from publishers as remuneration to the author. Let them give the royalty or not, I permit any number of publishers to come forward to print my books for wide circulation throughout the world. Usually they give me 100 copies for every 1000 copies published. I do not sell those copies and earn any profit. I distribute the copies to all important libraries, educational and religious institutions and to daily newspapers for purpose of review. This proves to be an efficient channel for publicity and the copies are sold out quickly and the publishers earn profit. I wish all should prosper.

I look to the spread of knowledge. Sitting in a small Kutir in the Himalayas on the banks of the

Ganga, I have published hundreds of very useful books in all languages for circulation throughout the world. This was possible, because I have not entertained any mercenary motive. My liberal views attracted many publishers in all countries like Germany, Switzerland, America and Indonesia. Some publishers do not like to handle valuable books on high Vedanta. They want to earn enormous profit by selling books quickly on Magic, Miracles and Yoga. Important works on Vedanta and Health are sold gradually, and hence the publishers are not so much interested in them. So I thought of having my own publications. In the interest of future generations, for preservation of valuable books, now I restrict the copyright of all my works to the Divine Life Society or the Yoga Vedanta Forest University. And yet I permit others also to publish my books.

Even if I do not demand any royalty copies, politely I tell the publishers in a convincing manner to give me some copies for free distribution. They give me 100 or 150 copies (per thousand) liberally. I call the 'royalty' copies as Ganesh Pooja, as offering to the Lord. In 1936, I wrote the following lines to a Publisher in India:

"Kindly remember the Ganesh Pooja copies. It is in your own interest. Whenever a tree bears fruit, the first fruit or vegetable should be offered to God or Sannyasins. Then the man prospers with grand success. Even so in regard to the Ganesh Pooja copies. The publisher attains prosperity, here and hereafter. I utilise the copies in bringing wonderful publicity for the books."

I am highly pleased if all the books are printed in

the University Press, as here I have full freedom. When copies are received from the press, I give away all the copies free to the inmates, visitors, pilgrims and, by post, to all devotees, Branches of the Divine Life Society and all religious and educational institutions. Daily I empty all the almirahs in the office, and yet I find fresh stock continuously coming from the Press. Now there are many devotees in all parts of India and Hong Kong who print large number of copies of my books and send me all the copies for such distribution. My joy is great when devotees send me contributions for this publication work and the maintenance of Sadhakas at the Ashram, or for the relief of the sick persons in the Hospital.

Attitude Towards Profit Motive

When there was some discrepancy in the accounts with a publisher, I asked one of my disciples to behave well and to maintain a cool mind. Some of the letters to him reproduced below will explain my attitude to the business people:

"Be calm and serene. Never fret yourself. Be magnanimous and 'Gambhira'. The whole world is yours, your body, your home. Be a Sakshi. Watch."

"Do not fight. Under all conditions, be polite, civil and courteous. Money is nothing. Be friendly with the publishers for ever. Become fearless. Have no quarrel with regards to the accounts. Be noble. Go on reasonable lines. If they are wrong, point out to them the mistake. If they persist and stick to their mistakes, keep silent. Ignore the whole matter even if we have heavy loss. Do not use any harsh word in your letter. Politeness and courtesy must breathe in every line. Settle the account without going to the courts. Consult a lawyer on the point. Do not lose temper. Act like a Sannyasi."

CHAPTER NINE

THE IDEAL OF LIFE

The Philosophy of Life

The aim of philosophy is right living. The meaning of right living depends on how it is defined. It is a life of wisdom, free from the imperfection, which characterises unphilosophical life. Philosophy is neither intellectual diversion nor aristocratic pedantry which overlooks the facts of experience in the world. As against a feat of scholarship or a mere hobby of the care-free mind, philosophy is the intelligent analysis of the implications of experience and a scientific theory evolved from such wise meditations for the purpose of regulating the functions responsible for the various experiences in the world. Philosophy is, therefore, the great art of the perfect life, a kind of life where the common notion of life is transcended and where the Supreme Life, which is identical with existence itself, is realised.

The philosophy taught by me is neither a dreamy, subjective, world-negating doctrine of illusion, nor a crude world-affirming theory of humanism. It is the theory of the divinity of the universe, the immortality of the soul of man, which is identical with the Absolute Self of the universe, there being an essential unity of everything in the universe with the highest Brahman, which is the only existing Reality. The Vedanta does not shut its eyes to the heart-rending, pitiable condition of the world, nor does it ignore the body and

(114)

the mind with their downward pull towards an empirical life, though the province of the Vedanta is supra-mundane.

Integral Development

The one Brahman or the Supreme Self appears as the diverse universe in all the planes or degrees of its manifestation, and, therefore, the aspirant has to pay his homage to the lower manifestation before he steps into the higher. Sound health, clear understanding, deep knowledge, powerful will and moral integrity are all parts of the process of the realisation of the Ideal preached by the Vedanta. I insist on an all-round discipline of the lower self. The teachings of the Vedanta are not in conflict with Yoga, Bhakti or Karma. All these are blended together as elements constituting a whole in the several states of its experience.

To adjust, adapt and accommodate, to see good in everything and to bring to effective use all the principles of Nature in the process of the evolution of the individual towards Self-realisation along the path of an integrated adjustment of the human powers, are some of the main factors which go to build up my philosophy of life To love all and to see God in all, to serve all, because God is all, to realise God as the identity of all in one fullness of perfection are the main canons. In all my writings I have prescribed methods for overcoming and mastering the physical, the vital, the mental and the intellectual planes of consciousness in order to enable the aspirant to proceed with his Sadhana without impediments towards this great spiritual destination, the realisation of the Absolute. The Vedanta is a philosophy and way of life which teaches the method of spiritual realisation, the direct experience of the immortal, the omnipresent nature of the Self, where the universe is realised as identical with the Self, where nothing second to the Self can exist, and as the result of this high realisation, the realised sage becomes the Saviour of the Universe, *Sarva-bhuta-hite Ratah.*

My Creed

To behold the Atman or Self in every being or form, to feel the Brahmic consciousness everywhere, at all times and in all conditions of life, to see, to hear and taste and smell and feel everything as the Atman is my creed. To live in Brahman, to melt in Brahman and to merge and dissolve in Brahman is my creed. By dwelling in union with Brahman, to utilise the hands, mind, senses and the body for the service of humanity, to sing the Lord's Names for elevating Bhaktas, to give instructions to sincere aspirants and to disseminate knowledge far and wide through books, pamphlets, leaflets, magazines and platform lectures is my creed.

To be a cosmic friend and a cosmic benefactor, a friend of the poor, the forlorn, the helpless and the fallen is my creed. It is my sacred creed to serve sick persons, to nurse them with care, sympathy and love, to cheer up the depressed, to infuse power and joy in all, to feel oneness with each and every creature and to treat all with equal vision. In my creed there are neither saints nor sinners, neither peasants nor kings, neither beggars nor emperors, neither friends nor foes, neither males nor females, neither Gurus nor Chelas. It is all Brahman. It is all Satchidananda.

Secret of Energy and Dynamic Work

I am now 72 (in 1958). I keep myself busy. I am always blissful and happy. I can do more work. I personally attend to hundreds of students at the Ashram and manage the affairs of the Divine Life Society, the Forest University, the General Hospital and guide thousands of students at far off places through correspondence. I pay much attention to the Printing Press and the despatches of useful books to the students, libraries and religious institutions. I can do more. The secret of my energy for the dynamic work is the keeping up of the Divine Consciousness throughout.

Change the angle of vision and be always happy and cheerful. See only good everywhere. Dance in joy. Saturate the mind with divine thoughts. You will at once feel tremendous, inner spiritual strength and spiritual power from within. The peace you enjoy now cannot be described in words. Adopt any method that can make your mind move inward, that can make the mind one-pointed and steady. Keep control over the senses. Have a careful vigil and intense faith. Develop will-power. Otherwise, Vikshepa and Alasya (oscillation and laziness) will overpower you.

Healing Through Prayers

All over the world, doctors experiment on the poor patients with so many medicines. How to expect a permanent and lasting cure when the doctors work with the selfish motive of earning more and more wealth? In the Ayurvedic system experts prepare genuine drugs from Himalayan plants, seeds and roots. They study the pulse of the patients and diagnose the case properly and prescribe effective medicines for bringing a permanent cure in the patients. The patients also should follow natural methods to a great extent and select suitable food-stuff and follow the instructions of the expert doctors.

In this Ashram I combine all the methods in the Sivananda General Hospital. There are expert doctors in all systems of medicine. In addition to this, I have great faith in the power of Mantra and grace of the Lord. Through special prayers conducted in the Lord Viswanath Mandir, I have seen miraculous cures of the hopeless cases even in distant places. I have tremendous faith in healing through prayers—healing of diseases by chanting of Mantras and prayers. The results are wonderful. The Lord's Name is so effective. I call this NAMAPATHY.

CHAPTER TEN

MY METHODOLOGY OF THE EVOLUTIONARY PROCESS

1. Detached, Yet Careful

In my Kutir, there are many big trunks with hundreds of valuable books, articles and dresses. I do not know the exact contents of the trunks. I do not have any keys with me. I do not keep anything as 'secret'. I cannot eat anything in private. I do not pretend to be a Vairagi with empty hands, expecting others to keep enough for my personal use. When I travelled on propaganda tours, I kept enough money with me in two or three pockets. I gave separate purses with plenty of money to those who accompanied me.

I am very careful in keeping things like fountain pen, spectacles, study books, and various articles contributed by all great men and devotees. Previously when I locked my Kutir for a short brisk walk, I kept the key carefully tied at the end of my cloth. I may use a torn coat with patches but I must give others the superior quality of articles. I do not worry about debts. I find necessary support spontaneously coming from the Divine Source. I feel the grace of the Lord at every step. I feel the presence of the Lord at all times, behind all names and forms.

2. Sadhana Till the End of Life

The Sadhus and Yogis do Sadhana and study for

some time and then give up the habit when they get a little name and fame. It is a great pity. That is the reason for their downfall. Sadhus and perfected Mahatmas should continue Sadhana till the last moment of their lives. Then only will it be possible to keep up the Divine Consciousness. That will be a fine example and a source of inspiration to others also. The saint need not talk and preach. His life itself is a scripture to illumine the world. Even today I write OM OM OM and HARI OM TAT SAT Mantras in all my letters. I fill up half a page of my letter with the Mantra or with philosophical ideas. Before commencing to write anything in a notebook or letters to students, I write the Mantra.

I do about five or six items of Sadhana all the 24 hours: Japa, meditation, exercises including Asana and Pranayama, worship, study, writing work and service to the world, help to Mahatmas, the sick and the poor. Thus I charge my mind with divine consciousness at all times. I nicely combine rest and relaxation with deep breathing exercises. I have thus spent my 35 years of life at Rishikesh and derived wonderful fresh spiritual energy and strength in abundance. I maintain a high standard of health and enjoy peace and bliss at every moment. I just come out of my Kutir for one hour in the morning and manage all the affairs of the Ashram and give work to those who live in the Ashram and think of others who live at distant places. And yet I feel I can work for another ten hours every day. The secret is my systematic Sadhana and the grace of the Lord.

3. Why So Many Photographs

In holy temples the authorities do not permit the

taking of photographs of the idols. In Badri and Kedar, people do not allow cameras to be taken inside the temples. It is strange. Some of the sages and great men of India have serious objection to taking their photographs. They think that the spiritual power will be diminished by taking photographs. I do not believe at all in such things. I allow anyone to take any number of pictures while sitting, running, walking, talking, eating, playing, swimming in the Ganga, in meditation, study or worship at the temple. When devotees look at a picture, they get inspiration. Books and magazines have a special charm with the addition of a series of pleasant and instructive pictures. I do not have any restriction. I find only good in every thing.

Great men from all countries come to the Ashram. Sincere devotees from all parts of the world come and stay with me for some months or years. They all desire to have a copy of my photo in their company. Why should I unnecessarily refuse and displease them? Groups of students who come to Rishikesh during vacation desire to have a group photo with myself in the centre. I have been photographed with the great men of the world, Maharajahs, sages and saints, devotees, Ashram workers, the sick persons in the Hospital and the school children. I have been photographed with my hat and suit, a loin cloth and an overcoat, with a turban like a school master, in a motor car, aeroplane and a bullock cart in Rameswaram during my All-India tour in 1950, and in a cycle-rickshaw during my stay at Roorkee in 1953. I make no distinction in having photographs with Maharajahs or devotees or coolies at the Railway

Station platform, with great Mahatmas of the Himalayas or the scavengers of the Ashram. I have included the lively monkeys, cats, dogs of the Ashram, fish, cows, elephants and cheetahs also. I do not believe in the statement that my spiritual powers will be lost or influenced by the evil-eye. I look at the wonderful benefits the world would derive. I enjoy when I find people around me feel happy and cheerful.

4. Self-reliance

I personally attended to my works such as, cleaning the room, bringing water from the Ganga for drinking purposes, washing clothes and vessels, going to the Kshetra for my alms. I myself used to type my articles and letters to aspirants. I carefully packed the packets and posted them. I never depended on my students. I did not like them to enter my Kutir frequently and disturb my daily routine. When I go out on tour, I myself carry my luggage. When porters carry some of my heavy packages of leaflets and books for free distribution, I pay them liberally. I pity those rich persons who fight with the porters and coolies at the platform for the sake of two annas.

When the work in the Ashram multiplied, I could not find time to attend to this kind of work. Sincere students came forward to attend to some of these works. As selfless service brings about purification of the heart, I permitted them to do this work and to serve other Mahatmas and sick persons. I carefully attended to the needs of the visitors and the inmates. I personally saw that they had their hurricane lanterns, (then there was no electricity), cots, beds, books for study, in their rooms and that they got their timely tea,

milk and food. Now hundreds of students have come
to the Ashram. Things go on in an organised method,
automatically. I silently sit, watch and enjoy the grace
of the Lord. I supervise every section of work and give
instructions to all the members and fix up able hands
in charge of all departments of work. Even people
without any ability or qualification, quickly pick up their
work in a short period when I give them full liberty and
responsibility and show confidence in them.

5. A Purpose Behind Everything

I am by nature serious. Even today I am very
serious in my Sadhana, study and service. Nothing
can disturb me from my concentration and peace. I
can remain blissful and attend to my work steadily
under all circumstances. Sometimes to elevate the
depressed, to cheer up the dull, I appear to be
humorous. I may joke and play with my students and
visitors and make them laugh like children. But,
behind every joke, fun and humour, there is a
purpose. I have a limit for everything. Every action or
word has a definite purpose in the evolution of the
people around me. Through fun and humour, through
presentation of biscuits, fruits and clothes, I find out
the taste, temperament and weakness of the students
and teach them a way to get over their difficulties and
defects.

I am dead against gossip, giggling and guffaw. I
ask my students to avoid loose talk and to live alone
with introspection or work. When they go out to bathe
in the Ganga or for meals or for a walk in the evening,
I ask them to go alone and to do Japa.

6. Simple Living and Generosity

I am economical. I do not spend much on my personal needs. I have lived for years a hard life by depending on the Kshetra food. I am very happy when I lead a rough and hard life. Simple living helps in high thinking and getting mastery over mind and body. Even today, I love the alms I get from the Kshetra and use torn clothes. I always hammer the mind with the words: *'Kaupeenavantah khalu bhagyavantah'*—Blessed are the dispassionate. I live in a rented building by the side of the holy Ganga, even though there are many palatial buildings in the Ashram with all comforts and conveniences. There is a special joy in simple living. But I do not suffer in the name of Tapas. When there is a need for certain items for the improvement of the Ashram or any individual's evolution, I insist on the needful being done immediately.

At every step I think of the welfare of the world and the evolution of the aspirants. When devotees give me valuable items and sweets with great devotion, I accept them with great love and affection. I use them to please the donors or give them away at once to deserving people. When I serve and help others, I want the best quality in everything. When I get a superior fountain pen, coat, a shawl or an easy chair, immediately I want to give similar items to all the workers and important persons in the Ashram. I await a chance to purchase the items, as in a growing institution where dynamic work is carried on with voluntary donation, it is difficult to find finance immediately. I wait for opportunities. I attend to the needs of all the inmates of the Ashram, one by one.

When I get sweets or fruits, I do not eat anything secretly in my Kutir. I carry the bundle to the Satsanga Hall and distribute them to the people assembled there and then take a small portion at the end as Prasad. Even with my diabetes trouble, sometimes I take a lot of sweets brought by devotees with so much of devotion, love and affection. I am not affected at all.

7. Not a Slave of Fashion and Style

I do not know fashion or style. This is a curse. I do not live for sensual enjoyment. It is the product of Maya, delusion, the way of the egoistic and the ignorant. I always wear my dhoti above my knees. From the way of dress, walk, talk and behaviour, I can easily find out the ego in different persons and prescribe methods to destroy it. Sometimes I wear a Turban and keep a long walking stick. In Swargashram when I had my evening walk, I kept the long walking stick. I used that as Yoga Danda for changing the flow of breath from one nostril to another and thus maintained the Swara Sadhana. In my earlier days I never used shoes or umbrella. One's attitudes, ways and manners become entirely different by the constant use of shoes, walking stick and umbrella.

8. Evolution for Everybody

Sadhanas differ according to the stage of evolution, the strength of ego, weaknesses and the nature of the lower Self. A strong and sturdy constitution and a fine health are in themselves a good qualification for the student. All other qualifications can be developed when one is placed in favourable environments. In the spiritual path any type of student can progress and evolve if he is endowed with Sraddha, sincerity and faith. There is no need for special talents or qualification. There is no need also for a deep study for years and Japa on one leg for decades. A willing, loving heart is what is needed. Scavenging, typing, writing, carrying water, nursing the sick, helping the poor—all these forms of service can be converted as YOGA with the right mental attitude. The student must have a new angle of vision and try to crush the ego at each step by discipline, discrimination and dispassion. Charge the mind with Divine Consciousness through constant Japa, prayers and systematic meditation.

9. Personal Attention and Liberal Disposition

The kitchen is the fighting centre in an Ashram. All sorts of troubles and misunderstanding, hatred and jealousy among workers, emanate from the kitchen. I can easily find out the taste, temperament and spiritual progress, and control of the senses of the students from the stories I hear from the kitchen side. That is the main centre of disturbance in an Ashram. But it is the best field for a quick spiritual evolution of the workers, for developing cosmic love, sympathy, mercy, patience, generosity. People are well trained to adjust and adapt themselves here in a marvelous way.

Due to the large number of inmates and the heavy rush of visitors, arrangement has been made for the supply of a common type of food in abundance, two or three varieties to suit the various tastes of the people of different provinces in India and of other countries. In a humorous manner I say to the people:

"If you do not get ghee, take milk. If milk is not available, ask for butter-milk. If this also is not obtainable, take plenty of Ganga water." They should not murmur. One has to be very cautious in adjusting and adapting to various circumstances if one wishes to enjoy peace. I ask them not to think much of their body or bread or beard. They all should constantly think of the all-pervading Brahman.

I pay special attention to supplying energising food and fruits to some of the workers in the Ashram who are busy with responsible work or intense silent Sadhana, to those who need more nutrition. I send special fruits, biscuits and butter to their own Kutirs. I serve them unasked. Their health must not suffer in the name of Tapasya. In the same manner, I carefully attend on the visitors also. They cannot change their habits in a day at the Ashram. That may affect their health and they cannot do any kind of Sadhana if they make a sudden, drastic change in their food and dress and relaxation. I do not, therefore, insist on strict rules and restrictions regarding diet for any one.

Even if there is some bad habit like that of tea, coffee and smoking, I allow them to continue their ways for some time. When they attain mental purity and will-power, all evil habits drop by themselves. The mysterious influence of the Ashram atmosphere has its own effect also. This sort of freedom given to the aspirants enables even a dull type of aspirant to feel quite at home in the Ashram and to plunge himself in dynamic work and develop his hidden faculties. Particularly in regard to the sick persons, I am very liberal. When fruits are not available in the local bazaar, I send a special messenger even to Delhi, thus spending a lot, for bringing oranges for the patients in the Hospital. A stitch in time saves nine.

10. No Compulsion But Full Liberty

I permit people to have their own ways and to work in any field suitable to their taste and inclination for some time, and create in them a natural taste for the right line of work and Sadhana. I do not compel anyone. Some of the letters I wrote in 1938 to one of my students will explain the method of my work and my consideration for the welfare and temperamental preferences of my students:

"You are in need of plenty of rest. You will have it as soon as the present work is finished. You need not work hard. There is no hurry. Take your own time. Do not worry unnecessarily about anything. I will take all responsibilities, mistakes, on my head. You need not worry anything about the activities of the Divine Life Society. Whatever little help you can do, you may do in future, if you want. You have done enough now. Be cheerful and happy. May I send you some more money for your expenses?"

"After finishing one or two books, you can return to Rishikesh. But one suggestion. Take rest for two weeks in a village. Completely stop all printing work. Then join the work. If you stay for a month or two, you can do some solid work. For two years you can remain in Rishikesh without going out. If your health permits, you can consider this point or come to Rishikesh at once. It is left to you to decide. Everything is left to your convenience and discretion."

"I will not connect your name with the Divine Life Society. You can help me if you want without any label, whenever you find time, whenever you like. You are ever free."

"I am marking, you are enslaving me through your real affection. Don't have any Moha for this body of mine. Become independent. I have made you free. I can help you more when you are away. I do not wish anyone to work with me for a long period."

"Don't be afraid of work. You can go to Uttarakashi next year. You need not attend to any work. But prepare and train able hands to continue your work. There are good persons here who are saturated with and absorbed in the typewriter. Pray, do not stop my book work. Let there be some series of books *ad infinitum*. I am sure people will run after my books for the practical lessons and guidance given there."

11. The Way to Get Things Done

In the past, I maintained a Memorandum notebook to enter the items of work I entrusted to various workers. I called this "WHIP". Even if due to pressure of work, students forgot the items, I did not leave them until the work was completed. Politely I used to remind them often. But this was done in a way humorous and charged with affection; and no one was displeased with me when I sent several reminders for the same work. For the Tamasic type of persons, I wrote stiff letters also, but at the end I added a few lines of advice to make them cheerful and happy. Some of the original letters are reproduced below. First I enquire about their health and spiritual progress and then ask about the work entrusted:

"How do you do? Do you keep up burning the Divine Flame, even amidst various activities in remembering His Name, feeling His presence everywhere, and seeing Him in all faces? Work hard. Meditate. Do Swadhyaya. Don't talk much. Don't mix. Don't be curious for news. Go for a walk alone in the evening. Do not neglect to maintain the Spiritual Diary. That is your Guru by your side. Write 'Hari Om' Mantra ten times at the top of your letters. This is an easy Sadhana for Self-realisation, remembering God during intense activities. Kindly take great care of your health. Be regular in your Japa, meditation and study. Change your nature and habit gradually.

"Hope you are keeping good health with Brahma Chintana, along with Karma Yoga. What about 'Science of Pranayama'? Is it ready? Why you are silent on this subject? Kindly send me a set of final proofs."

"I hope you are O.K. Have Smaran of Rama, Krishna or Siva along with your work. You will become a Yogi and a Jnani. This is easy Yoga for you amidst various activities. Draw inner energy and peace through silent meditation at least for a few minutes in the early morning. I have to reiterate again and again: World is a dream, Jaalam, jugglery of mind. It is Bhrama (mere appearance). You are Atman (Satchidananda). Assert. Deny body. With great effort get yourself established in this Bhav. Feel: 'I am One—Ekam, Chidakasa, Akhanda Brahman, the Self of all beings, I am Sakshi, I am Akarta.' Stamp out the hissing Indriyas and Vasanas. This is the Upanishadic essence—quite sufficient to destroy ignorance. Send me a report of how you spend all the "24 hours of the day, please."

I never forget the spiritual interests of my

students, and continuously remind them of the purpose of life and the importance of Sadhana, even though they may have a lot of work to do for the divine mission. Here is another letter:

"This world is Deergha Swapna. You are Vyapaka Atma. Be established in this one idea. I have to hammer on this point very often. Acknowledge the article; 'Sat Guru Mani Mala.' If you don't do this, reminders after reminders will be sent to you until I get answer. To avoid this boring, say: 'Yes, received Sat Guru Mani Mala.' This will save a lot of time and energy."

"I have written to you several times for compiling all my letters to you in a book form. Just a little trimming repeated portions and selecting of the lessons useful to aspirants. I have not received an answer from you. If you are not inclined to do this work now, I shall wait. This will not tax you much. You can do it slowly."

12. Message of Cheer

I don't believe in scandal-mongering. Pardon even the worst sinner. There is hope for everybody to improve and progress in the spiritual path. I want my disciples to be strong, bold and cheerful. I want them to carry on dynamically the mission of the Lord. My letters attest this attitude:

"Don't waste your energy in worrying unnecessarily. Our work is increasing by leaps and bounds. Shall we attend to the scandal and criticisms or proceed on with our Yogic activities? Forget. Forgive. Forgive.

"Even if people advertise you with a lady by your

side in daily papers, I won't believe. It is the mischief of scandal-mongers. Even if I catch you red-handed with a lady, I will excuse you. These are all mistakes only in the path and not heinous crimes. I will tell you, 'Don't do this in future. March on in the path of light.' You are unnecessarily bothering yourself. I wanted to send you a telegram to cheer you up. You have to do many ennobling works. I am preparing the ground, paving the way for your future spiritual activities.

"I wish many students like you will crop up in India to help the world. Be bold. Be always cheerful. Proclaim the Truth everywhere. Stand up. Gird up the loins and preach Vedanta, Yoga, Bhakti everywhere. Don't worry yourself even a bit. No one in the world can hurt. You are invincible. Roar like a lion on any platform, resting on Truth. The slight defects in you will soon vanish. Don't bother. In the Atman there is purity. It is Niranjan, spotless. Thou art Niranjan. Stick to this idea. The impurities will vanish. This is the positive method of eliminating or eradicating defects. Strength, joy, peace, bliss, immortality is your very nature. Assert and realise."

13. Attitude Towards Vilification

Here is a letter addressed in 1937 to one of my students who published a pamphlet attacking the Founder of a famous Ashram in Punjab:

"I came to know that you have published a small pamphlet wherein you have indirectly attacked an Ashram in Punjab. You ought not to have done this. It is vilification. Forget the past. It is not a noble act for a Sannyasi. Petty-minded householders only will behave like this. Sannyasa is magnanimity. In future don't do any thing of this kind. It indirectly affects me. How is your health?"

I want my disciples to mind their own business and not to waste their energy and time in cavilling at others. I want them to have a broad vision, to acquire balance of mind and cultivate the spirit of tolerance and forgiveness. The letter continues:

"Your work will suffer if there is even a little agitation. Keep silent and work with undivided attention. Have no connection with anyone. Let everything end peacefully. Forget everything. You are still very weak. You are swayed or tossed by 'words', jugglery. Become adamantine. 'Tit for tat' is the nature of householders and not Sannyasins. To bear insult and injury is the Svabhava of Sannyasins. That is spiritual strength. That is the balance. To be moved by trifles, to worry for months and to waste energy in a useless direction is not wisdom.

"Keep quiet. Never think of old affairs. You are wasting your energy by thinking in wrong directions. This will interfere with our smooth work. Stop selling the remaining copies of the pamphlet and destroy them. The Founder of the Ashram is my dear friend, brother. You must not do any thing that can affect him in the least even indirectly. You are conscious of certain harmful things that are written there. Forget everything. Rest in peace. Don't bring out any such books. Write purely on philosophy, Yoga, Bhakti and Vedanta. Don't bring out tracts of this nature. Even though you are in the right, when the other party is aggrieved, you must be sympathetic. Don't bring out such pamphlets even if you have good materials. Be careful. When the party feels a lot, how can you poke or rake up the matters again and again. It is not the Dharma of a Sannyasin. How long do you want to continue this sort of business? Keep the mind cool and direct your attention to our publications, meditation and other useful work."

14. Rise Above Criticism

I am not interested in useless arguments but am concerned only with quick action and obedience. I do not want my disciples to be upset by criticism. Hence my strong exhortation:

"This affair is serious. I want you to keep absolute silence in future. This needs your immediate action. I don't want to hear your arguments, justification, etc. The matter must be absolutely stopped. I may be partial and unjust. You need not send me a reply. But kindly see that you act up to my request immediately without fail. Sannyasa is for peaceful and constructive work. What more shall I write to you? Are you the Atman or the mind and body? Even if you have read 1001 times all my writings, still you identify yourself with the mind and the body. People can criticise your body and mind. You yourself dislike your body and mind. Those who criticise your body are your real friends. Then, why do you get agitated? You are weak. Ignore criticisms. Why do you brood over the past? This is a bad habit. You can't have peace of mind. Rise above criticisms and remarks. Do good to that man who wants to poison you and kill you. Put it into practice.

"You have learnt many things from that unhappy, unpleasant occurrence that was worrying you. It was in the grand plan for you to gain some experiences.

Out of evil comes good. It has given you strength and wisdom. Now rest in peace and work like a lion. Joy, Bliss, Power, Strength, Splendour and Glory are your Divine heritage. Think you are the emperor of the world. Face difficulties boldly. Draw inner strength. God has given you special favour. He has made you a Brahmachari and cut off all ties and made you absolutely free. Where then is room for lamentation, despair, sorrow, worry or depression? Smile. Cheerfulness, peace, divine service, Yogic activities, dissemination of knowledge, form part and parcel of you now. I am always at thy feet to serve thee. Be assured. Be assured. Be assured. Jump in joy. Dance in ecstasy. Walk like a lion. Radiate Joy, Peace and Strength to all around."

15. Constancy and Gratitude

I can never forget the services done to the divine mission by my disciples. Even if, for some reason or other, they go away from me, I do not forget the work done by them. They continue to live in my heart. The letter continues:

"Never change your opinion. I am thy servant, well-wisher, friend, brother. Even if you leave me, I cannot leave you. I won't leave you. You always reside in my heart. You are dear to me always. I cannot utter any harsh word to anyone. If anyone utters a harsh word, I feel for that man. I want to correct him. You may experience this. You might have experienced this. I am grateful to the Lord who has endowed me with at least a ray of this virtue. I do not crave for higher attainments. The Lord has given me this quality. It is His mercy.

"Now the whole matter is clear. Feel His Mercy and Grace. I am myself going to the Post Office and posting this letter. It is very difficult to understand the mind of a man even though you move with him very closely for years together, and to understand even one's own mind. God alone knows the real culprit. You know me full well by close contact. It would have been a nice thing to drop the correspondence concerning the bogus letter altogether and you ought to have talked to me about it privately when you come down here, even though you have reason, to suspect from the signature and the envelope. This is all unnecessary botheration to you, to me and to all. There is no time for you or for me to look into these matters and to waste our time and energy in these worthless topics. We should utilise every second of our life in His service and meditation.

"You ought to have had a strong belief that I will never write such a letter to you. You have failed here. It does not matter. Man learns and grows by mistakes.

"Even if a thousand people poison my ears and mind by speaking ill of you, I won't hear. You are glory to me, to India and to the world."

16. You Cannot Get Away From Evil

"This world is a strange world. We have to learn many lessons. One of the disciples of the Lord Jesus betrayed the Lord. Many obstacles will come to the growing aspirant at every step. We will have to show our strength. Do not be agitated by little things. Be cheerful. Smile. Walk boldly. Think and feel that nothing has happened. Don't worry about little things. You have to do many great actions yet. Prakriti is preparing you in a variety of ways. Feel this. Be grateful to the Lord.

"These things have happened, yet i cannot leave you or Sri 'B' or Sri 'A' or Sri 'Y'. All grow by committing mistakes and blunders. You must forget the past entirely. As I have written above, I shall arrange for your residence in Brahmananda Ashram and supply separate food for you. You need not mix with anybody. Some work you can do for the Divine plan. You cannot eliminate evil persons from any part of the world. Wherever you go, you will have to live amidst them. But have Atma Bhav. This will change the situation.

"You should try to love all, even the worst man who wants to destroy you. That is Sannyasa. A Sannyasin is one who feels that he has no body. We should live amidst people who want to destroy us, amidst unfavourable surroundings and then work and meditate. Then only can we grow. Then only can you have the unruffled mind of a Sage. For this you must have tremendous inner spiritual strength and faith through Sadhana."

17. My Attitude Towards Dissension Among Disciples

One of my students wrote a bogus letter with my false signature to another important worker at Madras. That disturbed and upset the person. Here is the letter showing my method of work for establishing peace and proper understanding. The letter was dated the 8th September, 1937. It clearly explains my attitude, the nature and method of my work. Even if the whole

Ashram is affected, I stick to my principle which is underlined as:

"I cannot hurt the feelings of anyone even in my dream. I love all, even the worst man who aims at my life. Even if students leave me, I cannot leave them. I unite the workers with my spiritual glue: '*Om Namo Narayanaya*' Mantra and Prayers."

Here is the complete text of my above-mentioned letter outlining my attitude:

Beloved Sri Swamiji,

Pranams. I have not written any such letter to you. It is a forged letter. Kindly compare this signature very carefully with others. You will find out the thief. Kindly send me the letter per registered post for my perusal. I presume it must be a typed letter. Can you make out whether it is typed in our machine or any other machine, and by whom in our group?

Some days ago there was a trouble here. Swami 'B' created some mischief. So I have asked him to leave the Ashram. Sri Swami 'A' and 'R', his friends, also have left the place. They are all living now in Rishikesh. They have planned this mischief to create some ill-feelings between you and me and to drive out Sri Swami 'Y', their enemy. This is their plan, I presume now. Sri 'B' is deadly inimical towards this Ashram and somebody has set fire to the bed of Sri Swami 'N' also.

You ought to have understood immediately: 'Swamiji will never write such a stiff letter. Possibly it is some mischief by others.' Everything will be all right. Be not troubled. When you come here, you can live separately in Brahmananda Ashram. You need not take meals from our kitchen. I shall make special arrangements for your food. As soon as the work is over, come here immediately. You need not wait even for a single moment. Do not worry a bit about the forged letter. It is the mischief of scandal-mongers. He who does wrong action will reap the fruits thereof. The law of Karma is inexorable. I wanted to send you a wire: 'Don't worry. It is forgery. It is a mischief by someone. Letter follows.' Then I thought a detailed letter would explain matters clearly."

18. Raking Up the Issue Does Not Solve Problems

I do not usually entertain complaints. There will be no end for the arguments given by different groups of persons. I know well that an enquiry will worsen the situation. Just for the satisfaction of the persons concerned in the 'plot', I made some enquiries on the subject and gave my conclusions in the letter reproduced below. I allow 'time' to improve the situation. The letter continues:

"I called this morning all the inmates of the Ashram and enquired into the matter. No conclusion has been arrived at. God only knows the real truth. I have no clairvoyant powers to find out the culprits. You can judge yourself as to who the culprit is. Can you make out the real man from the style of typing? Even if you spot out conclusively, the man will not admit. Do not feel a bit anything now. Be cheerful. Everything is false; some mischief has been done out of jealousy. It is very difficult to find out the mischief-makers. You need not come here soon, if there is work there, on account of this perturbed condition of mind caused by this affair. Be cool. Do sufficient work. Collect all the rays of the mind and be calm. Forget the past. Do as much work as possible. Plunge yourself in work. Do not be agitated. These little difficulties and disturbances come in the way to strengthen you, to strengthen me. We should not be disturbed. All these matters happen only to make us strong. It is all for your growth and improvement only.

"One thing I have found out; you become agitated soon. As soon as I read your letter, I was extremely surprised. I could not make out to whom you were writing, because I never wrote to you anything of the kind. Even if you have found out that to be my signature even if the envelope was bearing my own handwriting, you should have thought that someone has done a mischief. Even supposing I have written such a letter, I would have done it for your own good or for the good of some one. You have hopelessly failed. I cannot hurt the feelings of anyone, even in dream, even that man who is injuring me to the extreme. I am developing this one virtue. Be sure of this always, even if such things happen in future."

19. Way to Success

Whenever I take up any work,
I finish it at any cost.
Whenever I start writing a book,
I complete it somehow or other.
Whenever I take up a book for study,
I complete it before taking up another work.
I never leave anything half done.
I concentrate on the subject and
Think intensely without distraction.
I am firm, steadfast and steady.
I have intense application to work.
I have tenacity and intensity of purpose.

20. How to Convert the Nature of a Man

Honour those who are bad characters. Serve the rogue first. Treat him as a future saint, as a saint, as a saint himself. This is a way to purify your heart and to elevate him also. I take a special delight in serving such people carefully. I always keep around me any number of people who would abuse me, vilify me, insult me and even try to injure me. I want to serve them, educate them, elevate them and transform them. I address them in the most respectful terms. Acclaim the rogue or the thief as a saint and publicly honour him, he would be ashamed to continue his evil doings. Persistently tell an ill-tempered man: "You are a Santa Murti (a man of peace),"—he would be ashamed to lose his temper. Call a lazy man, "You are a dynamic worker," and he would throw off his laziness and plunge into service. This is my method. The praise should come from the very bottom of your heart. You must give your soul-force to every word. You must sincerely feel that behind the apparent negative quality, there is a resplendent positive virtue latent in the man. Then both of you will be benefited.

21. My View of Goondas

Good people are already virtuous
I will have to correct and mould Goondas only.
This is my special work.
Goonda is a negatively virtuous man.
He exists to glorify the virtuous.
Goonda also is Lord Krishna.
Lord Krishna says in the Gita:
'Dyutam chhalayatamasmi—
I am the gambling of the cheat.'
Rudri says: 'Taskaranam pataye namah—

Prostrations the Lord of thieves,'
I keep in the Ashram all sorts of students.
The world calls me a Guru for thieves and rogues.
Glory to the Divine Mission.
The spiritual vibrations of this Holy Centre
Convert them as Divine Beings, Yogis and Saints!

22. Destroy Abhimana (Egoism)

It is well to remember that Sattva, Rajas and Tamas have their own "hooks" that keep the Sadhaka back and prevent him from soaring into the realms transcendental. The Sattvic hook is the most subtle of all and therefore most difficult to discern and detect. With Sannyasa, floats the Sannyasa Abhimana. It might allow the student a greater freedom to roam a little higher than others, but he is also bound. With Tyaga, creeps in Tyaga Abhimana, most subtle and most dangerous, almost impossible to get over. Similar is the case with Seva-Abhimana. Egoism takes many shapes. Sannyasa, Tyaga and even Seva is transformed by it into its cloak. The Sadhaka who would like to strive for realisation of the Self would do well to guard himself well and not allow quarters to these subtler forms of Abhimana.

23. An Ideal Teacher

I am ever a thirsting student
I am not a teacher
But God has made me a teacher
The students have made me a teacher.
I make my students soon as teachers
I am such a teacher.
I treat them in respectable terms as
'Maharaj', 'Swamiji', 'Bhagawan', 'Narayan',

I treat them as my equals
I give them equal seats
I am such a teacher.
I allow them to learn from my own life
I make them Mahants and servants of humanity
Presidents, lecturers, writers, Swamis and Yogis
Founders of spiritual institutions, poets, journalists,
Propagandists, divine scavengers, health
    and Yoga Culturists,
Typists, Yoga-kings, Atma-Samrats,
Karma Yogi Veeras, Bhakti Bhushans,
    Sadhana Ratnas
I am such a teacher to all Seekers after Truth.

24. Come, Come, My Friends

My Call is irresistible,
It has transformed countless lives.
Do not waste this precious life
In playing cards and idle gossiping
Give up hot debates and arguing
Destroy all pleasure centres
Abandon the desire for comfort
Set fire to the fuel of lust.
Destroy the fortress of egoism
Be quick, Be quick, friends!
Sing the Lord's Name day and night
Now take a plunge in the Ocean of Bliss
And enter the illimitable domain of the Atma within.
Come, come, my friends, take the plunge, be quick
Tarry not, delay not—enjoy the Wisdom Bliss.

CHAPTER ELEVEN

PRACTICAL HINTS ON THE SPIRITUAL PATH

1. Training of Students Through Post

I have no stereo-typed, printed lessons in Yoga for coaching up students through post. I usually send some of my books suitable to the taste of the students. I give them lessons through correspondence. The lessons are well graded. They write to me about their daily routine, welfare and progress. They maintain the Spiritual Diary and follow my "Twenty Important Spiritual Instructions." I help them with advice and remove their troubles and obstacles. I send my thought-currents of peace. Thousands of students in all countries have made wonderful progress through this personal attention. For the advanced courses they come to the Ashram and stay with me for some weeks or months and receive initiation.

They all like this kind of individual attention. I do not take any fees from any one for the training given in Yoga, and do not demand any money for their maintenance at the Ashram. Invariably all students who come to me pay me liberally or take pleasure in voluntarily contributing their mite to the progress of the institution and helping the Society in its dissemination of knowledge. Through such acts, they obtain Chitta-Suddhi and spiritual progress.

In the following pages are reproduced some of my typical letters to different aspirants, delineating the

(144)

methods of my training in the path of Yoga, the spiritual perspective. I emphasise to all, the moral and ethical ideals. I exhort others to emulate—in short, showing the way to lead the divine life.

2. Way to Peace

Swarg Ashram,
16th August, 1930.

Revered Brother,

Your kind line. Thank you very much indeed. Get up at 4 in the morning. Have a meditation room under lock and key. Do not allow anybody to enter it. Have a Gayatri picture, the Gita, etc., in the room. Meditate on the Gayatri. Repeat the Gayatri Mantra with meaning. Concentrate on the Trikuti, the space between the two eye-brows, with closed eyes. Sit on Padma-Asana. Try to sit for two hours continuously. Study the Gita regularly. Speak the truth at any cost. Control anger. Serve poor persons, the sick and the saints. Spend some money on charity. That will purify your heart. Don't join worldly persons. Serve, love, respect everybody. Give up Ninda (criticising), back-biting, fault-finding, tale-bearing. Be humble. Be obedient. Speak sweetly. You will enter into Peace. Observe Mauna for one hour daily and three hours on holidays.

Yours fraternally,
Swami Sivananda

3. Have Strong Thirst for Knowledge

I advise aspirants against emotionalism and impetuosity in taking to the path of renunciation, but counsel diligent cultivation of a strong urge for spiritual life while yet in the world.

Swargashram, Kutir 22,
29th August, 1930.

Om Sat-Chit-Ananda,

You are the Atma. You are immortal. Be fearless.
Assert the majesty of your Self. Free yourself from
the deceptions of the mind and worldly objects.
My Dear Yogi, May God bless you.

I am filled with infinite delight to peruse your line of
the 21st instant. You are a man of spiritual
Samskaras. Nurture them. Protect them. Increase
them.

DO NOT COME TO ME

If you can manage, and if you are quite sure that
you will not become a menace to society, if you can
control lust, be a Brahmachari till the end of life
(Naishthika Brahmachari). You are not rich. How can
you manage a family and children? That will bar your
spiritual progress.

Mere juvenile enthusiasm will not do. Mere
emotions will not do in the spiritual line. It is not a rosy
path. It is full of thorns, scorpions and snakes. The
path is rugged, precipitous, extremely difficult, but
easy for a man of the strong determination: "I must
realise—I will give up life even." This kind of strong
thirst for Knowledge is needed.

Develop Sattvic virtues gradually—patience to
counteract anger, contentment to check greed, service
(Seva Bhava) to destroy pride, arrogance. Develop
humility, truth-speaking, Titiksha (bearing heat, cold,
pain). Love all. Be kind to all. Never become irritated,
excited. Keep a diary of spiritual progress. Record
everything. Live amidst developed persons. Visit the

Ramakrishna Mission and serve the Mahatmas. Serve elders with enthusiasm, love and affection (deep). Clear your doubts. Wishing you peace and beatitude,

Yours

Sivananda

HARI OM TAT SAT
OM SANTI!

Get a copy of my Yogic & Vedantic Sadhana.

In future send me a reply post card or postal envelope for my reply.

4. Do Not Be Hasty in Leaving the World

c/o. Vizianagaram House,
Camp/Calcutta,
12th December, 1930.

OM SAT-CHIT-ANANDA

Come to Rishikesh for some time. You will enjoy the solitude and the spiritual vibrations undoubtedly. Tell my name. People will accommodate you and serve you. Have Darshan of Sri Swami Advaitanandaji, Sri Swami Tapovanji Maharaj, Sri Swami Purushottamanandaji. They are all in close touch with me,—advanced souls.

Do not be hasty in leaving the world. The world is an arena for developing various Sattvic qualities. The world is the best teacher for those who want to be benefited. Remain for some time longer there. Earn and enjoy. Vairagya comes out of Bhoga. Then it will be strong, steady and intense. DO NOT MARRY. That is a different point. The world is not a hell. It is all Ananda when ego and Raga-dvesha die away. Change the mental attitude. Come and see all these places and Mahatmas. You will have inspiration.

Lead a divine life when you are there. The spiritual path is not all rosy. It is full of thorns. Qualify yourself. Attain purity and spiritual strength through Japa and meditation. Cheer yourself.

Wishing you Kaivalya Moksha,

Swami Sivananda

Hari Om Tat Sat
Tat Tvam Asi

5. Look Before You Leap

The preceding two letters, addressed to one of my disciples, would show how I caution aspirants against any hasty decision. But when I find that one is endowed with strong Vairagya and unshakable determination, I am at once filled with joy and delight. On those days, when I lived alone and had no Ashram of my own, I was very reluctant to have any disciple by my side. I did not want anybody to come and stay with me. Hence, in the case of the above-mentioned aspirant, when I found that he had strong aspiration and unwavering will, I felt that it would be better for him to stay in an active Ashram, so that he might improve there rapidly. Thus I preferred forgoing my own interest by not availing myself of the services of aspirants, and always looked to their own welfare and the progress of other religious institutions.

Beloved Self,

Your devotion towards God and religion will doubtless elevate you from Samsara. May God bestow on you spiritual strength and power to attain the Goal of life—God-realisation.

Kindly join Sri Aurobindo Ashram or the Ramakrishna Mission. There you will improve a lot. I promise you. I assure you. Stick to the Ashram for some years. You may come here for visiting and not for permanent stay. LOOK BEFORE YOU LEAP. Think. Consider well. The world is the best teacher. You have to learn a lot. Do not be hasty and run away to the Himalayan caves. Youthful buoyancy, juvenile enthusiasm, may not help you much. This line is an arduous, hazardous path. You may not know how to spend your time usefully here.

I am only a common Sadhu. I may not be able to help you much. Further, I do not make disciples. I can be your sincere friend till the end of my life. I don't like to keep persons by my side for a long time. I give lessons for couple of months and ask them to meditate in some solitary centres in Kashmir or Uttarakashi.

I reiterate: Join a good Ashram where you will have spiritual gain. Stick to the centre. Bear difficulties. The end is immortality, infinite Ananda.

Thy Own Self,
Swami Sivananda

Cheer yourself. Be free, courageous, fearless. You are Nectar's son. Hari OM Tat Sat. Develop patience. Speak the truth. Control anger. Develop Titiksha. Serve. Love. Give. Forgive others. Speak a little. Speak sweetly.

6. Snippets for Evolution

Here are some valuable instructions in tablet form—succinct to the point and sorted out for immediate application.

Swargashram
3rd October, 1930.

(a) Fear not.
(b) Grieve not.
You are Sat-Chit-Ananda Rupa, Amrita Atma.
You are not this Jada body.
May God bless you.

Kindly go through my book: "Mind, Its Mysteries and Control." The lessons will be of much practical use for progress in meditation. Save as much money as possible. In these days money is needed even by Sannyasin, as there is lack of support from householders. Have these two important pleasure-centres: STUDY and MEDITATION. Cut off all external pleasure-centres.

1. Search. Understand. Realise.
2. Analyse (objects). Realise (their true nature) and abandon.
3. Know Thyself and be free.
4. Always be Self-centred.
5. Pray and be virtuous.
6. Aspire and draw.
7. Negate (body) and Assert (Brahman)
8. Tat Tvam Asi—never forget this.

SIVANANDA

7. Unfold the Latent Divine

True to my advice, the aspirant joined the Ramakrishna Mission, and yet continued to be in touch with me. I did not deny him my constant care and instructions for evolution, as I consider all Ashrams my own and do not recognise any exclusive monopoly over any aspirant who approaches me for guidance:

Swargashram,
Rishikesh.

Revered Brother,

Om Namo Narayanaya. May God bless you.

I have returned from a long Kailas trip. I am glad to hear that you have joined the Ramakrishna Mission. My heartfelt congratulations. Stick to the Ashram with leech-like tenacity. The Ashram is your own. Feel this. You are bound to progress. You are the Sun of suns. You are hope of the world. You have taken a responsible gown. Unfold the Divinity. May holiness, splendour, glory attend on thee.

You have cut asunder all the earthly ties. Now you can proceed unhampered in your way. Stick to the Mission and serve all your elders with respect and sincerity and disinterestedness. Speak the truth at any cost. Speaking the truth cannot harm anybody. It will give you spiritual power. Truth can be achieved only by speaking the truth. Control anger by developing patience, Kshama, cosmic love, service and Daya. You must cultivate humility, magnanimity (Audarya) and courage.

Six hours of study and six hours of meditation should go on uninterruptedly. That is my method. Forget the past. Live in the solid present. Give up all kinds of fancied expectations. Even if people persecute you, hate you, mock at you, keep quiet. Don't revenge. Study the 'Sermon on the Mount' daily before you proceed to work. I shall quote one passage. If you remember this once daily you will have wisdom. Practise this unceasingly:

'Love your enemies. Bless them that curse you. Do

good to them that hate you and pray for those who despise and persecute you.'   —St. Matthew.

The practice is difficult but must be done and can be done. This is being practised by Mahatma Gandhi. This is the secret of his success.

With regards and Prem,

Your humble brother
SWAMI SIVANANDA

8. Regeneration of the Lower Nature

In spite of my reluctance and initial objection when the aspirant subsequently came to me and made a strong impression about his spirit of renunciation and adamantine will-power. I willingly initiated him into the Order of Sannyasa, and he immediately plunged himself into the arena of the divine work, which was then in its initial stages and which was soon to assume gigantic proportions and astound the world with a tremendous whirlwind of spiritual revival and divine inspiration among millions of aspirants all over the world. Yet, I never forget the object of life and the purpose with which one renounces the world, and, therefore, repeatedly exhorted him to pay attention to practical Sadhana and self-discipline:

SIVOHAM SIVAH KEVALOHAM. May God bless you.

I have great hopes in you. You are a glory to India and the world at large. May the Divine Light, Divine Splendour and Glory shine in you for ever. Live in Truth. Feel Truth. Realise Truth. Disseminate Truth. Regulate your energy. Conserve it. Utilise it when needed. Meditate well. Live in a closed room. Don't mix much. Do not multiply friends. One real and sincere friend is quite sufficient. Don't beg with the begging spirit. Command and get whatever you need. The whole world is your home. Prakriti and nine Riddhis are ready to serve you with folded hands. Control Indriyas. AWAY FROM LADIES. Be fiery. Don't become a lazy *Zenana* Vedantin or a moustache-lady Sannyasin. There must be fire in every cell, in every word. I know you will do wonders within a short time. Read the Upanishads and the Gita. Master them well. You are a zero in that direction.

You should have regular, systematic study, meditation and Japa. Don't think: 'I will study in Uttarakashi when I am alone without work.' That is wrong. That is foolishness. You must have the daily habit. That 'tomorrow' will never come. Make hay while the sun shines. Winnow the corn when the wind blows. Concentrate. Meditate. Live alone for some hours. Be polite. Never be arrogant. Have tolerance and patience. Manifest these virtues while talking. Watch every thought. There is no play. You have taken a responsible garb. Do you feel this? Away from ladies. No joking and laughing with them. These are all manifestations of lust only.

Don't beg. Don't ask with the begging spirit. Command. Everything will come. The whole world is your own home. Feel this. Feel this. Show me a report of your systematic Sadhana. Method and discipline must be there in your daily routine. Scrutinise your motives. Destroy selfish motives. Crush all sorts of meanness. Become noble in every inch of your action. Don't fight for petty trifles. Give up back-biting, tale-bearing. Regeneration of the Asuric nature is imperative.

OM
SIVOHAM

9. The Bane of Sensual Life

I once again emphasise the importance of Sadhana and the necessity of shielding oneself from the baneful effects of a sensual life:

Don't look at the filth again. Don't ruin yourself. You have sufficiently enjoyed a life of joy and bliss in the spiritual path. What to speak of further glories if you blossom fully through Yoga. Beware. Beware. Don't become a slave to your senses. Don't come out of your room. Stop all activities. Hide yourself in a room or come back to Ananda Kutir at once. Introspect and meditate.

❀   ❀   ❀

If you cannot resist Moha, it is better you leave the city at once. Proofs will take care of themselves. I do not care for work at all. If you are strong enough, you may stay there for some time more and finish the work. Anyhow make arrangements for coming to Rishikesh soon.

❀   ❀   ❀

Without ideal life, resting in the indwelling, interpenetrating Presence, sensual life becomes a burden. It is tantamount to brutal life. The world is a dream. The Essence is the solid Reality. Never forget this. You are the Atma, Akarta, Sakshi.

10. Sadhana Should Be a Daily Habit

The following are some of the important hints on the path of Yoga which are culled from my different letters to aspirants, and which will be found very useful to one and all for a correct knowledge of some of the practical aspects of the spiritual path.

You should have regular, systematic meditation, Japa, study and service. Don't think: "I will study and meditate when I finish all my responsibilities, when I am alone in the Himalayan Caves." Live alone for some hours and study the mind. Prepare now slowly for the life in seclusion.

11. Nishkama Seva

This does not require big funds. If you are fit to serve humanity, the Lord will arrange everything for you. Get some useful medicines and distribute to the sick persons or nurse them nicely. Do not expect anything from anybody for the service you do. Give education to the poor boys in your village. Maintain yourself by getting alms from 4 or 5 houses. Live in seclusion. Do Sadhana. Destroy Manorajya, building castles in the air. It is an enemy of peace. Do service according to your ability, capacity and means, as much as you can, with the right mental attitude and spirit.

12. Troubles Through Pranayama

I have received similar reports of troubles from many students who try to awaken the Kundalini Power by forcible methods of Pranayama and Kriya Yoga. I pity them for their over enthusiasm and incomplete knowledge. Reduction or giving up of food may not help you at all. The field must nicely be prepared by regular daily practice. In the advanced stages you must have the personal guidance and supervision of the elders who have attained mastery and perfection in the path of Yoga. Purity of heart, congenial company, correct understanding of the scriptures, favourable atmosphere and environments charged with spiritual vibrations play a vital part in your quick success. Do not be hasty or impatient. One-sided development will not help you. Do not spoil your health by too much fasting. That will weaken your system. Take plenty of energy-giving, easily digestible, nutritious food, and fruits and milk. For some months, breathe in and out very, very slowly. Do not retain the breathe (Kumbhaka). When you advance a bit, move to a cool place during summer and have three sittings in Pranayama. Follow the proportion 1:4:2 for inhalation, retention and exhalation. The benefits are incalculable. It is a harmless exercise for advanced students.

13. Overcome Depression and Gloom

Run in the open air. Do mild Pranayama. Chant OM. Sing with devotion. Dance in ecstasy. Depression will vanish soon. You are Ananda Svarupa—where is gloom and depression? They are mental creations only. Remain silent. You can gain more by silence. Soak a few Badams (almonds) overnight in water. Take them in the early morning with sugar-candy. It is very efficacious as a brain-tonic for Sadhakas. Apply Amalaka oil on the head. Take Huxley's Syrup also.

14. When You Are Agitated

Do not leave Japa and Sadhana even for a day. Adjust and adapt. Bear insult and injury. Learn to forget trifles. Tactfully move with people. Train everyone in Bhajan and Kirtan. Create spiritual vibrations wherever you go. Then you will find peace, joy, happiness and prosperity. There will be joy in all laces. This is the way for harmony. When you are agitated and irritated, take to Japa or leave the place for some time. Love all and serve all.

15. Avoid Extremes in Yoga

In Yoga exercises, do as much as you comfortably can. Avoid extremes. Do not tax yourself. People in foreign countries find it difficult to do Padmasana (folding the legs in lotus pose) and Sirshasana (head-stand pose). For prayers and meditation, you can have any comfortable position. You must select a fine pose in which you can sit for a long time comfortably. The only condition is that your neck and back should be erect. Close your eyes, breathe in and out very slowly and mentally repeat the Mantra OM OM OM and think of the divine qualities of the Lord. Now you will enter into silent meditation. You will enjoy great peace and acquire inner spiritual strength.

16. What Is Actual Yoga

Yoga does not consist in sitting cross-legged for six hours or stopping the beatings of the heart or getting oneself buried underneath the ground for a week or a month. These are all physical feats only. Yoga is the science that teaches you the method of uniting the individual will with the Cosmic Will. Yoga transmutes the unregenerate nature and increases energy, vitality, vigour, and bestows longevity and a high standard of health. Try to increase the power of concentration. Japa will help you to have a one-pointed mind.

CHAPTER TWELVE

SPIRITUAL EXPERIENCES

1. Dawn of New Life

I was tired of this illusory life of sense-pleasures
I became quite disgusted with this prison of body.
I had Satsanga with Mahatmas
And imbibed their nectarine instructions.
I crossed the dire forest of love and hatred.
I roamed far beyond the world of good and evil
I came to the border-land of stupendous silence
And caught the splendour of the Soul within
All my sorrow is over now
My heart is now brimming up with joy
Peace has now entered my soul
I was suddenly lifted out of my life
There was a dawn of new life.
I experienced the inner World of Reality
The Unseen filled my soul and heart.
I was bathed in a flood of effulgence ineffable
And saw the Lord behind all names and forms
And realised that I am the Light.

2. Preliminary Spiritual Experiences

More and more dispassion and discrimination,
More and more yearning for liberation,
Peace, cheerfulness, contentment,
Fearlessness, unruffled state of mind,
Lustre in the eyes, good smell from the body;
Beautiful complexion, sweet, powerful voice,
Wonderful health, vim, vigour and vitality,

(158)

Freedom from disease, laziness and depression,
Lightness of body, alertness of mind,
Powerful Jatharagni or digestive fire
Eagerness to sit and meditate for a long time
Aversion to worldly talks and company of worldlings
Feeling of Presence of God everywhere
Love for all creatures,
Feeling that all forms are forms of the Lord
That the world is Lord Himself
Absence of Ghrina or dislike to any creature
Even to those who despise and insult
Strength of mind to bear insult and injury
To meet dangers and calamities
Are some of the preliminary spiritual experiences.
These indicate that one advances
In the spiritual path.

II

Balls of white lights, coloured lights
Sun, stars during meditation
Divya Gandha, Divya Taste,
Vision of the Lord in the dream
Extraordinary, superhuman experiences,
Vision of the Lord in the human form
Sometimes in the form of a Brahmin
Old man, leper or out-caste in rags
Talking to the Lord,
Are the preliminary spiritual experiences.
Then comes cosmic consciousness or
        Savikalpa Samadhi
Which Arjuna experienced.
Eventually the aspirant enters
Into Nirvikalpa Samadhi
Wherein there is neither seer nor seen
Wherein one sees nothing, hears nothing
He becomes one with the Eternal.

3. I Have Won the Game of Life

Through the Grace of the Lord and Sat-Guru
I am unattached and free.
All doubts and delusions have vanished.
I am free and ever blissful
I am free from fear,
As I rest in That non-dual State.
Fear is due to duality.
I am Brahman-intoxicated.
I have attained perfection and freedom.
I live in the pure consciousness.
I have won the game of life.
I have won! I have won!! I have won!!!

4. In Him I Find My All

At last His Grace descended on me
I gazed and gazed at Him
I was lost in that wondrous Vision of the Lord.
The Grace filled the cup of my heart.
The ecstatic thrill overwhelmed me
In His Will is my peace
His Name is a heaven of repose
In Him I find my all.

All knowledge is locked up in His bosom
The whole creation rise and fall in Him
He is the Supreme Reservoir of all that appears.
He is the Mainstay of all the worlds.
He is the Holy One, Perfect in Wisdom,
The cause of this world, the Bestower of Salvation!

5. In the Ocean of Bliss

O Mahadeva, O Kesava
By the sword of Thy Grace
I have cut off all my bonds
I am free, I am blissful

All desires have disappeared
Now I aspire nothing
But Thy blessed Feet
I have lost all my thoughts
In Thee, O Narayana.

I had Thy wondrous vision
I was lost in ecstasy
I was at once transformed
I was drowned
In the Divine Consciousness
In the ocean of bliss
Hail, Hail, O Vishnu, My Lord.

6. Immortal Self I Am

One eternal, infinite Being alone exists
Jiva is identical with this Being
Pain is unreal; it cannot exist
Bliss is Real; it cannot die.
Mind is unreal; it cannot exist,
Soul is real; it cannot die.
Freedom comes through knowledge of the Self
Freedom is Perfection, Immortality and Bliss
Freedom is direct realisation of the Self
Freedom is release from births and deaths
I am neither mind, nor body
This whole world is my body
The whole world is my home
Nothing exists, nothing belongs to me
Immortal Self I am.

7. Speechless Zone

In the perfect nameless, formless Void,
In the unlimited expanse of bliss,
In the region of matterless, mindless joy
In the realm of timeless, spaceless, thoughtless space

In the transcendental abode of Sweet Harmony
I united with the Supreme Effulgence
The thought that we are one or two vanished
I crossed the sea of birth for ever.
This is all due to the Grace of the Lord
Who danced in Brindavan with rhythmic jingle
Who raised Govardhan as umbrella for the cowherds.

8. I Have Become That

The Maya-made world has vanished now
Mind has totally perished
The Ego has been entirely powdered
The watertight compartments have been broken down
Names and forms disappeared
All distinctions and differences have melted
Old Jivahood has entirely fused
The flood of Truth, Wisdom and Bliss
Has entered everywhere in abundance
Brahman alone shines everywhere
One homogenous Joy-essence pervades everywhere
I have become That. I have become That.
Sivoham. Sivoham. Sivoham.

9. The Great Bhuma Experience

I merged myself in great unending joy
I swam in the ocean of immortal bliss
I floated in the sea of Infinite Peace
Ego melted, thoughts subsided
Intellect ceased functioning
The senses were absorbed
I remained unawakened to the world
I saw myself everywhere
It was a homogeneous experience
There was neither within nor without
There was neither 'this' nor 'that'

There was neither 'he', 'you' nor 'I' nor she
There was neither time nor space
There was neither subject nor object
There was neither knower nor knowable nor sight
How can one describe this transcendental experience?
Language is finite, words are impotent;
Realise this yourself and be free.

10. Mysterious Experience

Brahman or the Eternal is far sweeter than honey
Jam, sugar-candy, Rasagulla or Laddu
I meditated on Brahman, the Immutable
I attained the stage that transcends finite
True light shone In me
Avidya or Ignorance vanished in toto
The doors were totally shut
The senses were withdrawn
Breath and mind merged in their source
I become one with the Supreme Light
A mysterious experience beyond speech indeed
Sivoham, Sivoham, Sivoham, Soham
Sat chit-ananda Swaroopoham.

11. Sivoham—Sivoham—Sivoham

I have realised the identity
Of individual soul and Supreme Soul
Sat-chit-ananda is my essential nature
My mind is withdrawn from all external objects
I am deeply God-intoxicated

All sorrow and pain and fear have vanished
I am ever peaceful and joyful
I am Truth, Pure Consciousness and Bliss
I shine forth as a Divine Flame.

In all living beings
I am tasting the Bliss of the Eternal

I have attained the Goal of Life
In that Brahman am I!

That Brahman who is Satchidananda
Who is the Indweller and Inner Ruler
Who is the womb of the Vedas
Who is the creator of this universe
Who is the substratum for everything
Who gives light to the intellect
Who is hiding himself in all forms
Who is adored by the Rishis
Whom the Vedas proclaim
Whom the Yogins wish to attain Samadhi
Who is terror to Indra and Agni
Who is sweet to the disciplined Yogi
That Brahman verily am I
Sivoham Sivoham Sivoham!

12. State of Samadhi

O What a Joy! What a Bliss!
All desires are now fulfilled
Everything is attained
I am Immortal, deathless,
I am Eternal Consciousness
I am the Great and the High
All this is mere Moksha
Moksha alone is everywhere
It is to be known
And experienced by everyone.

That ego has melted now
The Vasanas are burnt up
In the fire of wisdom
There is Manonasa
Or annihilation of mind
All distinctions have vanished
All differences have disappeared

There is neither 'I' or 'you'
All indeed is Brahman
This is one homogeneous bliss
This experience-whole is ineffable
Words fail to describe this state
Feel it yourself in Samadhi.

13. Through the Grace of Guru

I know my essential nature
I have reached the peak of perfection
I am pure Immortal Atman.

All my desires are gratified
I am Apta Kama
I have attained everything
I have done all my works

I have nothing more to learn
The Vedas have nothing to teach me
The Smritis have nothing to instruct me
The world has nothing to attract me

Maya is hiding herself modestly
As I know all her tricks and ways
She blushes to appear before me

This is all due to the Grace of the Lord
And the Grace of the Guru
He made me like Himself
Prostrations to the Guru
Obeisance to the Guru!

14. I Am That I Am

Timeless and spaceless is this goal
Painless and sorrowless is this seat
Blissful and peaceful is this Abode
Changeless and boundless is this Dhama
I know that "I am He"

I have neither body, mind nor senses
I have neither change, nor growth nor death
I am the Immortal, All-pervading Brahman.

Neither virtue nor sin can touch me
Neither pleasure nor pain can affect me
Neither likes and dislikes can taint me
I am Existence-Absolute, Knowledge-Absolute
    and Bliss-Absolute.

I have neither friends nor enemies
I have neither parents nor relatives
I have neither home nor country
I am that I am. I am that I am.
I am never born, I never die
I always exist, I am everywhere,
I have neither fear of death nor fear of public criticism
I am Siva, full of Bliss and Knowledge
Chidananda-rupah Sivoham, Sivoham.

CHAPTER THIRTEEN

WISDOM IN HUMOUR

The following excerpts from my letters to an aspirant clearly portray my temperament which is at once humorous with flashes that convey a deep philosophical bent of mind and extreme tolerance of other people's defects and weaknesses combined with broad liberalism and a profound understanding of the habits of people and the nature of things:

1. Training of Students in Lecturing

"You will have to lecture at least for 5 minutes in English and Hindi and do Kirtan also with Nritya whether your body is willing to bend and move or refuses to move. If there is difficulty in lecturing, kindly cram a few lines from my books. If cramming also is difficult, read from a piece of paper. If you show or exhibit your foolish obstinacy like a child, there is no other course for me than to carry you and put you on the platform. Don't give room for this extreme manoeuvres in these cold days."

Many students were turned into wonderful orators and Kirtanists after such compulsion by me in the early stages. I want everyone to be a fiery lecturer. People should learn to express their thoughts.

2. The Way of Business People

"In Samaradhana or Brahmana Bhojana, leaves are spread at 10 o'clock in the morning but the food is served at 4 in the evening. The same is the case with the PRACTICE OF YOGA. Advertisement has been going on for 5 weeks now and yet not even a smell of the book for me. The first fruit of a tree is always offered to God. The first bound copy should reach me by registered post. But when V.P.P. orders are executed in full, a residue copy is sent to me. This is the way of business people."

3. Regarding A Strong Packing Case With Thick Nails

"Thy parcel received in due order. It was a Brahman packing with Brahmic screws which had Brahma Nishtha. Hammering was not able to remove the cover. After all it was broken into pieces. Thanks* to the Brahmic packer of the parcel. The books reached me in good condition."

4. When Important Points Are Omitted by Publishers

"I have given you full permission or power of Attorney to remove whatever portion you deem fit to remove by your new long razor, just to suit your purpose in making the book grand and thrilling, but pray, keep a small tuft—according to Narada Parivrajaka Upanishad. Do not remove even a single important word from my writings, even if you find it a repetition."

5. Care About Manuscripts

I think you say 'goodbye' when the book RAJA YOGA is over. You will not be able to take up BHAKTI YOGA. Just as Sankirtan cannot enter your ears, so also this BHAKTI YOGA does not attract you much. I know that you will not take up this work. Kindly bring the manuscripts with you very carefully. I shall transfer it to some other press, in Northern India.

6. On Attractive Advertisement

The Advertisement of Vol. II of PRACTICE OF YOGA at the end of the book is not a thrilling one. It is quite ordinary. It does not give a full, select exhibit. You have nicely done before for YOGA ASANA, KUNDALINI YOGA, etc. Why not for this? Perhaps the Thermos Flask was empty.

7. Philosophy Over the Call of Coffee

The Winter of Rishikesh is sending invitations. You may be feeling the cool breeze also. The stove which was sleeping is now turning its face towards the Railway Station to receive you with great joy. He who throws light on the Winter season and the stove is the Self-luminous Para Brahman, the support for seasons and all names and forms. He never drinks and talks. He is Asanga. He is Sakshi always. Feel His Presence.

8. Method of Sending Reminders

Kindly advise me by a postcard: "Yes. I have despatched books for Libraries" or some code word. That will save much time and energy. It will not surely interfere with your deep Mauna. It is not Kaashtha Mauna or Maha Mauna. It is a form of 'Hu-Hu' Mauna.

9. Correcting the Ways of Students

Take special care of Poorna. My respects to him. He is simple, quiet and noble. Let him keep off his castor oil or quinine face.

10. Invitation for Formality

Kindly come to Ananda Kutir after fixing up everything there. Invitation for Birthday is just for information but 'not to come.'

11. Over the Damaged Parcel of Cashew-Nuts

Received Kajoo (cashew-nuts) in a damaged condition on account of the admixture of sugar-candy in hot summer. The candy has melted and made the Kajoo soft, which will be nice for veteran Swami Jnanananda. My teeth are quite sound and strong. In future do not send sugar-candy with cashew-nuts.

12. Rich Despite Debts

"Everyday new spiritual aspirants are coming to the Ashram. Hundreds of students write to me from all countries for spiritual guidance and I spend a lot in giving prompt replies to all the letters. Some Kutirs are under construction. Work is progressing on all directions. One cow is coming to the Ashram. You can take good milk. We are becoming rich nowadays despite debts."

13. Ideal Tonic for Brain-workers
(An Attack on the Coffee Habit)

Take Badams (almonds) and Huxley's Syrup. Put Badam oil or Amalaka oil on your head. This is very good for brain-workers. There is no 'Pathyam' —(restriction) on diet. Yon can take the same quantity or even more of Coffee.

14. My Respectable Guests

Received all letters and parcels of coffee. The first respectable guests for the 'tin' of coffee were Sri Swami Omkar who carried the bundle from the

Railway Station, and Sri Swami Poorna who prepared the coffee. Probably barber Balla will be my next guest.

15. An Attack on Weakness in 'Walking'

The Divine Life Society may send you as the head of a group of Sannyasins and Brahmacharins for propaganda, Kirtan and lectures if all goes well. Even in that case you will have to walk 12 miles a day.

16. Ways of Virakta Mahatmas

Your friend, that Mauni, Virakta boy of Swargashram who was with a towel only, has asked me to request you to send him one pound of snuff. This is also a kind of Vairagya. The nose has become like a machine-gun through repeated usage of snuff. He brings his ingenious arguments for his using the snuff. You can send him a small tin. Let this be your charity towards a Virakta Mahatma.

17. Philosophy Over Snuff

Snuff parcel received and distributed among:

1. Mukhya—chief snuffer   Sri 'V'
2. Adi Snuffer—Guru snuffer   Sri 'N'
3. Sanatan snuffer—old snuffer   Sri 'G'
4. Maha-snuffer—terrible snuffer   Sri Mauni
                        and Tyagi of Swargashram.

You will get some Punya and Papa also. I will also get a share, a small portion of Punya for relieving a bit of their suffering, Papa for making them continue their habit. Had we not supplied snuff, their habit would have been destroyed. But 'Aham Brahma Asmi people' are above Papa and Punya. So you are now freed by knowing your own Svarupa.

GLOSSARY

Acharya—Preceptor

Advaita—Non-duality, monism

Akarta—Non-doer

Akhanda—Unbroken, continuous, partless

Alasya—Inertia, Idleness

Ananda-bhashpam—Tears of bliss

Arhats—The perfect souls

Asana—Yoga exercises

Ashram—An ideal centre for Sadhana, a monastery

Bandha—A group of exercises in Hatha Yoga; a bondage

Bhagavatas—Those illumined souls who recite the stories of the Lord

Bhaitak—An Indian physical exercise

Bhajan—Praise of the Lord, singing in chorus songs in praise of the Lord

Bhakti Yoga—The Path of devotion

Bhakti—Devotion

Bhav—Feeling of devotion and love

Bhikkus—Monks

Brahma-muhurta—The period from 4 to 6 in the morning which is highly favourable for spiritual practices

Brahmachari—A Celibate

Brahmacharya—Celibacy

Chitta—Mind-stuff, subconscious mind

Dand—An Indian physical exercise

Darshan—Insight, seeing the Lord or holy persons

Daya—Mercy, compassion

Devas—Celestial beings, Gods

Dharma—Righteousness

Dharmasala—Charity house

Dvaita—Duality

Ekadasi—The 11th day of full-moon or new-moon, a holy day for observance of fast

Gambhira—Dignified, grand, magnanimous

Grihastha—Householder's life, a householder

Grihasthi—A householder

Guru—Preceptor, Teacher

Indriyas—Senses, sense-organs

Ishta-Devata—A particular incarnation of the Lord which appeals most to a person

Jaalam—Jugglery

Japa—Repetition of the Name of the Lord

Jnana-Yajna—Dissemination of knowledge

Jnana-Yoga—The path of knowledge

Jnana—Wisdom

Jnani—A Vedanti, one in the path of knowledge, the illumined

Kaashtha Mauna—Silence wherein one does not make even gestures and signals

Kamandalu—A vessel used by Sadhus for carrying water, mostly the shell of a hard fruit

Karma-Yoga—The path of selfless action

Karma—Action, fate

Kirtan—Loud singing of the Name of the Lord in different tunes

Koran—The holy scripture of the Mohammedans

Kshama—forgiveness

Kumbhaka—Retention of breath

Kutir—Hermitage, hut or cottage, where a renunciate or Yogi lives

Likhita-Japa—Writing of Mantras or the Name of the Lord

Mahant—The Founder or the president of a religious institution

Mahatmas—Great men, holy persons, high souled ones

Mantra—A sacred formula expressing obeisance to the Lord

Mauna—Observance of silence

Maya—Illusive power of the Lord, which is responsible for ignorance and bondage

Moha—Attachment to things and beings

Mudras—A group of exercises in Hatha Yoga

Mukti—Liberation, release from the bondage of birth and death

Mumukshutva—Intense longing for liberation

Murti—Image, an idol

Mutt—The institution of monks, a monastery

Namaskar—Prostation

Nirguna—Without attributes, the Absolute Reality

Nirvana—Final emancipation, liberation

Nirvikalpa Samadhi—Complete absorption in Reality; A state wherein one's identity with the Universal Reality is realised

Nishkama—Selfless service, work without selfish motive

Nishtha—Deep meditation; full dedication to a holy undertaking

Nivritti Marga—The path of renunciation

Parivrajaka—A Wandering monk; a mendicant

Pooja—Worship

Prabhat Pheri—A religious procession early in the morning

Prana—Vital force or breath in the body

Pranayama—Breathing exercises; Regulation of the vital breath

Raga-Dvesha—Feelings of attachment and aversion

Rajas—One of the 3 qualities producing passion and restlessness, the principle of dynamism in nature

Sadhaka—An aspirant; a spiritual practitioner

Sadhana—Spiritual practices

Sadhu—An anchorite

Saguna—The Absolute conceived with form; A personal God

Sahaja-Avastha—Superconscious state that has become natural and continuous

Saiva—The worshipper of Lord Siva

Sakshi—Witness; the self who acts as a witness

Samadhi—Superconscious state

Sammelan—A Religious Conference

Samsara—The process of worldly life through transmigration

Samskara—Impressions in the mind

Sannyasa—Renunciation

Sannyasi—A Monk

Sastra—Scriptures of the Hindus

Satchidananda—Existence, knowledge and bliss; an expression suggesting the Indescribable Absolute Reality

Satsanga—Association with the wise and sages

Sattva—Purity

Sattvic—Pure

Seva—Service

Shat-Sampat—Sixfold virtues: Sama (balance in pain and pleasure), Dama (control of senses), Uparati (tranquillity), Titiksha (forbearance, bearing heat and cold), Sraddha (faith and sincerity) and Samadhana (balanced state of mind)

Siddha—A perfected sage

Siddhi—Psychic powers

Svabhava—one's own nature
Svapna—Dream
Svarupa—Form
Swami—One who is devoted to the path of renunciation
Tamas—Ignorance, inertia
Tapasya—Austerity, penance
Titiksha—Forbearance
Trataka—Steady gazing
Vaikuntha—The abode of Lord Vishnu
Vairagi—A man of dispassion
Vairagya—Aversion to sense-objects
Vaishnava—Worshipper of Lord Vishnu
Vanaprastha—Householders leading a life of a hermit
Vedas—Scriptures of the Hindus
Vikshepa—Tossing of mind
Viraja Homa—Religious rite for entering the Order of
    Sannyasa, the path of renunciation
Viveka—Discrimination
Vyapaka—All-pervading
Yajna—A sacrifice
Yoga Bhrashta—One who has fallen from the high
    state of Yoga
Yogi—An aspirant going through a course of spiritual
    discipline, A student in the path of Yoga
Zenana—womanfolk